GOD OR MAMMON?

GOD
OR MAMMON?

The Snare of the Prosperity Gospel

Robin Compston

THE WAKEMAN TRUST, LONDON

GOD OR MAMMON?
The Snare of the Prosperity Gospel
© Robin Compston, 2018

THE WAKEMAN TRUST
(Wakeman Trust is a UK Registered Charity)

UK Registered Office
38 Walcot Square
London SE11 4TZ

USA Office
300 Artino Drive
Oberlin, OH 44074-1263

Website: www.wakemantrust.org

ISBN 978 1 908919 88 5

Cover design by Andrew Owen

Printed by Stephens & George, Merthyr Tydfil, UK

Contents

1 – An essential warning

WHO WOULD HAVE predicted that Christian churches would be infected by teaching as blatantly unbiblical as the Prosperity Gospel, an error which contradicts head-on the tenth commandment, and to which all believers should have an instinctive aversion? Yet this teaching has made strong headway, and its chief promoters are highly acclaimed even in churches claiming to be Bible-based. How do we explain the success of this movement and why are so many people enthusiastic defenders of its ideas? We have to conclude, while there may be many of God's true people in the affected churches, prosperity doctrines have been skilfully designed to appeal to the tastes of those who have never fully turned their back on the world, and who are susceptible to a message which offers them the possibility of serving both God and mammon at the same time.

The Word of Faith movement is a development within Pentecostal churches which is now in its second or third generation. The modern leaders of this movement trace their ideas back to such men as Kenneth Copeland, Frederick Price, and Kenneth Hagin, and beyond these to Oral Roberts and E. W. Kenyon. The Word of Faith movement promotes the Health and Wealth Gospel, or the

Gospel of Success, the wealth side of this message being known as the Prosperity Gospel. Teachers within the movement vary in their doctrines and in some cases are critical of each other's ideas; nevertheless, we see a core teaching which is held in common by most in this movement.

Prosperity teachers say that Christians should aspire to be rich in this world, for it is God's will that his people are blessed materially as well as spiritually. They say that a large part of Christian happiness comes from being well provided for in this life, which is taken as evidence of God's favour. Taboos against covetousness, which all previous generations of Christians taught, are dismissed by these teachers as enslaving scruples which cause unnecessary deprivation to believers, and rob the churches of resources needful for the evangelisation of a lost world. Poverty is blamed on the devil, and escape from this state comes through the practice of 'positive confession' by which words spoken aloud lay claim to material enrichment in the expectation that God will make this a reality. A strong connection is made between the practice of tithing and the receipt of an earthly reward, so that financial giving is regarded as a seed sown which reaps an earthly benefit in kind.

It might seem unwise to write a book that takes seriously teaching as outrageous as this, but there are true believers who suffer for many years before escaping its clutches. For the sake of genuine believers trapped in this movement, and to resist its harmful influence, this book examines the key teachings of the Prosperity Gospel in the light of Scripture.

2 – Rejecting past Christian teaching

It is readily admitted by prosperity teachers that their doctrine is a departure from the traditional teaching of the church on the subject of wealth. Far from being embarrassed by this, they pride themselves on discovering a truth hidden from previous generations.

In an effort to get Christians to change their thinking Kenneth

Copeland protests –

'Through our traditional ideas, we have been led to believe that prosperity is ungodly.'[1] 'Christians have avoided prosperity like the plague
because they have been taught that it would defile. But prosperity will
only result in destruction when the one who seeks it is without the
fear of the Lord and without the wisdom of God.'[2]

Leroy Thompson Sr. adds –

'The Body of Christ has suffered tremendously by being ignorant of God's laws of prosperity and of God's will concerning their
prosperity.'[3] 'The devil has told the Church that people who are
wealthy are worldly because they have so much.'[4] 'The church has
been all messed up about what God thinks about money.'[5]

Thompson offers to assist –

'Let me help you cleanse your mind so you don't have any religious
thinking left ... The Word gets all the religious, stingy, poverty, poor-
mouthing spirits out of you.'[6]

Often past Christian attitudes to wealth are criticised as extreme.
Kenneth Hagin attacks what he takes to be false humility –

'Many Christians equate humility with poverty. One preacher once
told me how humble another was because he drove a very old car. I
replied, "That's not being humble – that's being ignorant!" Driving an
old car was that preacher's idea of humility.'[7]

Frederick Price complains –

'Over the centuries, the devil has distorted all teachings on money
every which way he could to keep Christians from letting God prosper them ... First, he has persuaded some Christians that no action
at all is needed on their part to acquire wealth. Second – his favourite

1 Kenneth Copeland, *Prosperity: The Choice is Yours*, p23, Kenneth Copeland
Publications, 1985
2 Ibid., p39
3 Dr Leroy Thompson, Sr, *Money Cometh!* p7, Ever Increasing Word Ministries,
1996
4 Ibid., p10
5 Ibid., p14
6 Ibid., p16
7 Kenneth E. Hagin, *The Believer's Authority*, p47, Faith Library Publications, 1986

tactic – has been to try to convince Christians that money is bad and that being wealthy is sinful.'[8]

Describing the early history of the movement Price complains –

'The devil had done an excellent job of concealing the nature of riches, the principles of prosperity, and the life of abundance from most Christians. We didn't get a change in these deceptions until some fifty years ago when Oral Roberts first broke through into mainstream Christianity.' *[Price explains that Oral Roberts presented healing as a covenant right.]* 'Ministers ... began to look for other rights under our covenant. Only then did you start to see people discovering that prosperity on God's terms was one of those rights. The devil had succeeded for almost two thousand years keeping this quiet.'[9]

Describing past attitudes, T. D. Jakes also sees a need for change –

'The old saints who taught us back then had nothing, so it only seemed right to preach that having things was of the devil and that those who had things were living opulent lives now, but were going to burn in hell for that success ... They sang with sincerity the verse "I'd rather have Jesus than silver and gold, I'd rather be his than have riches untold." ... The world evolved, but they remain steeped in antiquated concepts that were reflective of slavery and poverty ... It was their sluggish mentality that kept them shackled to the past and their poverty ... How much more impact these good Christians could have had if only they had availed themselves of the riches the world offered.'[10]

But making a virtue out of poverty has never been the mainstream Christian attitude to wealth. Bible Christians have not linked piety to either wealth or poverty. Besides, this is a deceitful line of reasoning, because the great aim of the Prosperity Gospel is not merely deliverance from poverty, but a deliberate longing for and seeking after wealth, and in many cases extreme wealth. To pretend that poverty is the issue allows these men to misuse Bible texts which speak of God providing for our needs.

---

8 Frederick K. C. Price, *Prosperity: Good News for God's People*, pp 124-125, Faith One Publishing, 2008
9 Ibid., p 131
10 T. D. Jakes, *The Great Investment*, pp 14-15, Berkley Books, 2000

T. D. Jakes claims that the root of the older view is in monasticism and its ascetic practices in embracing poverty –

'This same philosophy moved from the hallowed walls of monasteries into the country churches on backwoods roads of farming towns across America.'[11]

But this is nonsense, because the avoidance of covetousness comes from the Bible and also from the Protestant Reformation. Faithful teachers of the past warned of the danger of covetousness because they were aware that the old nature is a tinderbox that still resides in the believer. They refused to ignore this major area of obedience to God, to which an entire commandment is devoted. They remembered all too clearly the examples in Scripture of those who were brought down by this sin. They were well aware that it is not money but the love of money that is a root of evil, and, realising this, they would do nothing to encourage the deliberate pursuit of wealth. They saw this world and all that belongs to it as passing away, and they believed true riches belong to the world to come. They taught that although the Christian may use this world's goods both for private enjoyment and the extension of God's kingdom, he reckons his treasure to be in Heaven and knows that to the extent that he lays up treasure on earth, he undermines his love for Heaven, and drags his heart down to earth. How different this is to the approach of prosperity teachers who urge their congregations to think highly of this world's goods and acquire all they can in this life.

3 – Appealing to claims of private revelation

What is the authority for the tremendous change in attitudes that the Prosperity Gospel seeks to bring about? We will look later at attempts to justify this teaching from the Bible, but for many of these teachers the great change in their thinking came not from the Bible, but through claimed personal revelation. God supposedly gave them

11 Ibid., p13

a vision which was to be shared with the churches and this quickly became the dominant theme of their ministry.

Kenneth Hagin relates a conversation which he claims to have had with the Lord –

> 'Then the Lord said, "For whom do you think I made the cattle of a thousand hills? For whom do you think I made the world and the fullness thereof? For whom do you think I made the silver and the gold – for the devil and his crowd? No! For my man Adam. But Satan came along and Adam committed high treason and sold out to the devil!" I had never heard anybody preach this. Back in January 1950, this was brand-new to me – a revelation!...The Lord said, "I'm not withholding adequate food and clothing from your little children – that's not me! It's the devil. He's the god of this world. The money you need is down there on earth; it's not up here in heaven."..."What should I do?" I asked. He replied, "...Claim whatever you need...You say, 'Satan, take your hands off my money!' Because it's Satan who is keeping it from coming to you – not me."'[12]

Hagin adds that Jesus told him that the angels are ministering spirits sent to serve believers. They had been standing around idle because Hagin had never turned in his order. He should have said, 'Go, ministering spirits, and cause the money to come.'[13] This absurd rewriting of Scripture *(Hebrews 1.13-14)* came through imagined private revelation.

Leroy Thompson's supposed revelation was straight to the point –

> 'More than a year ago, the Lord gave me this revelation of "Money cometh." At first, I thought He gave it to me just to bless me and my family, because "Money cometh" began working mightily in our lives...But soon after I received the revelation and saw what it was doing in our lives, God began dealing with me about sharing it with the body of Christ.'[14] 'The Father told me in my spirit, "I want you to have financial power, for if you get financial power, the power of My Gospel will be able to go to the four ends of the earth because you are going to give."'[15]

---

12 Kenneth E. Hagin, *How God Taught Me About Prosperity*, pp14-17, Faith Library Publications, 1985

13 Ibid., p19

14 Thompson, *Money Cometh!* p7

15 Ibid., p25

Thompson wants to share with us a revelation he was given during one meeting –

'Those who let Me do it for them, I'll do it swiftly, says the Lord. They'll be out *[of debt]* before they know it. Yield to My Spirit. Yield to My Word. Yield to My will. Yield to My way, and you'll see just what I say.'[16]

He explains that each believer needs to be personally convinced of this message –

'You see, you can realise mentally that prosperity belongs to you, but until you get a revelation – not from man but from the Holy Ghost – that God wants you to prosper, you will not arrive at a place of financial prosperity in your life.'[17]

Notice that the individual has decided in advance what revelation God is going to give him. When it comes, it just happens to agree with prosperity teaching, regardless of what Scripture says!

Matthew Ashimolowo expresses his confidence that the church is about to enter a phase of prosperity –

'In the past 40 years major ministers and ministries have been speaking of the coming wealth transfer *[from the world to the church]*. This includes the likes of Dr Oral Roberts, Kenneth Copeland and Dr Kenneth E. Hagin. In more recent times, the voices of people outside of the Word of Faith movement have been added to this prophecy.'[18]

We see how many errors flood in once professing Christians accept the notions of modern-day prophets. These writers are guilty of attributing prophetic status to their imaginations, claiming to have had revelations which fail the first test of true prophecy, since they contradict what God has already written in his Word. The revelation of Scripture closed long ago, the Bible being a complete revelation of all that we need to know about God, and about how believers should live their lives. God may guide us personally by

---

16 Ibid., p191
17 Ibid., p196
18 Matthew Ashimolowo, *The Coming Wealth Transfer*, p10, Matthew Ashimolowo Media Ministries, 2006

enlightening us about the meaning of Scripture, but he does not add new doctrine. It is alarming that large numbers of people trust these prophecies that give them false expectations of enrichment in this life, and present a God who leads his people into the danger-ous trap of covetousness.

4 – Teaching myths about creation and the Fall

One building block with which the Prosperity Gospel is constructed is the idea that God gave mankind all the riches of the earth at creation. Frederick Price employs a typical piece of simplistic reasoning saying that God –

> 'created all the gold, all the silver, all the diamonds – all the things that have constituted material wealth through the ages...If God created all this wealth, is it bad?...There is no poverty in God!...If you get poverty, it isn't coming from God, because God is the originator of all wealth in the universe.'[19]

According to Price, if God is the Creator of all wealth, it follows that he wants to give that wealth to man, if only man will tap into that wealth by faith.

In Prosperity Gospel teaching, what happened in the garden of Eden is that man placed himself under the tyranny of the devil, whose plan was to deprive man of the wealth that God intended to give him. Price says –

> 'Our enemy, Satan, has arranged the world system to allow you to have just enough money to get by.'[20] 'The dominion of the earth passed, in order, from God to Adam to Satan. For God to legally act in this world, he has to act through mankind, who were originally given dominion...As we will see, one of the main purposes of Christians being prosperous is to regain control of the world's wealth out of the hands of the devil.'[21]

Frederick Price rejects the clear teaching of God's Word that man's

---

19 Price, *Prosperity: Good News for God's People*, pp 13, 22
20 Ibid., p40
21 Ibid., p70

disobedience was punished by God's taking away the original blessing and benefits.

The same twisted thesis is taught by Leroy Thompson –

> 'God wants the body of Christ to take back what the devil has stolen.'[22] *[The wealth that God originally gave to mankind has been stolen. God wants to give it back to the church but the devil tries to prevent this.]* 'God wants His children to enjoy prosperity. Those nice restaurants were built for us! If anybody ought to be eating that steak and lobster, it ought to be the Lord's children! The devil's children have been in those nice places too long. It's time for God's children to be there.'[23]

To speak of God being rich in terms of silver or gold or anything else that he has made is utterly misplaced, for no Christian should measure the riches of the infinite, eternal, and all-powerful God in terms of created elements. 'The Lord is high above all nations, and his glory above the heavens' *(Psalm 113.4)*.

Although God gave man dominion over the works of his hands, man did not have that dominion immediately, for he was given the task of subduing the earth. There was work to be done even in his original state of perfection. Adam was set in the garden of Eden to dress it, the creation not instantly yielding all its treasures to him. Nor was man's dominion expressed in terms of the possession of silver and gold, but of dominion over nature: 'over the fish of the sea, and over the fowl of the air, and over every living thing that moveth upon the earth' *(Genesis 1.28)*.

The most precious things to Adam were not the riches buried in the ground, but his walk with God as he enjoyed communion with him in his original state of uprightness. His attention was supremely taken up with the Lord, then with the wonder of the gift of life, and of the world in which he found himself. God has indeed crowned man 'with glory and honour' and made him 'to have dominion over the works of thy hands' *(Psalm 8.5-6)* but as the writer to the

---

22 Thompson, *Money Cometh!* p9
23 Ibid., p122

Hebrews explains, 'Now we see not yet all things put under him. But we see Jesus, who was made a little lower than the angels for the suffering of death, crowned with glory and honour' *(Hebrews 2.8-9)*.

The promises to have dominion over the earth, including the enjoyment of all its treasures, are fulfilled in Christ and at no time since the creation of the world have they yet been fulfilled apart from him. Christ by his death and resurrection has earned the right to be heir of all things, and he enjoys dominion now, but for his people these blessings are still in the future. The saints shall inherit the earth for we are joint heirs with Christ, but we will not receive the inheritance until we are glorified together with him *(Romans 8.17)*. In other words the enjoyment of the inheritance must wait till after we are raised from the dead at Christ's return. Therefore it is a great mistake for prosperity teachers to argue that man has always had available to him all earth's riches.

It is not true that when Adam sinned he handed control of earth's riches to the devil. It was God who cursed the earth, not the devil; the devil also being subject to the terms of the curse along with man. It was God who drove man out of the garden of Eden and set a flaming sword to prevent him returning. Therefore it is a serious distortion of the Bible to say that God is somehow hindered by the devil (as Price claimed) from giving silver and gold to any as he wishes.

The Prosperity Gospel account of creation also ignores what has taken place since creation, namely the Fall of man into sin, which has made him prone to idolatry (serving created things rather than the Creator). God did not leave him to enjoy the original creation in this fallen state, but cursed the earth so that man was deprived of much of the enjoyment of its original glory. Scripture teaches that the most important thing man was deprived of at the Fall was not wealth, but fellowship with God, and the glory of the reflection of God that had been created in him, which was now desecrated by sin. These are the things that man lost, and these are the things that he is taught to long for, not money and wealth: 'Blessed are they which do hunger and thirst after righteousness: for they shall be filled' *(Matthew 5.6)*. Never does Christ mention the possibility of regaining earth's wealth as a motivation for men and women seeking him or wanting to enter the kingdom of Heaven.

Certainly, the devil robbed mankind at the Fall and took something that did not belong to him, and it is true that Christ restores this to us. But what Satan took was not the earth's silver and gold but something far more precious. Scripture teaches that what he took from us was our souls, and it was these that Christ set free by his atoning death on the cross. 'When he ascended up on high, he led captivity captive' *(Ephesians 4.8)*. Satan, who had held man in hopeless captivity, was forced to release his captives. Christ came 'that through death he might destroy him that had the power of death, that is, the devil; and deliver them who through fear of death were all their lifetime subject to bondage' *(Hebrews 2.14-15)*. Restoration of earth's wealth to the church is not worthy to be mentioned among these momentous achievements.

Christ did indeed purchase all things for his people, but we do not receive all the fruits of his redemption at once. We are immediately justified, and receive a new nature; we receive the earnest or downpayment of the Spirit, but the redemption of the body comes later. Now we must experience many of the trials of this life in common with all men including, at times, poverty. But when the kingdom of Christ comes visibly, then we will receive all. Paul says in *Romans 5.17* that we will reign in life, but he uses the future tense.

5 – Distorting God's covenant with Abraham

In an attempt to strengthen their case, Prosperity Gospel teachers argue that God has promised wealth to his people in the covenant made with Abraham, and that all the benefits of this covenant are transferred to the church in our day. Often, these writers have a confused view of the Abrahamic covenant and teach that Abraham enjoyed very different blessings from those given to the church.

Frederick Price says bizarre and unbiblical things about Abraham –

> 'Abraham was a servant of God – he could not be a son of God because Jesus hadn't died and been resurrected yet, so [he] had no way into the family of God.'[24] 'Abraham could not be blessed spiritually because Abraham, like Adam after his sin, and like every other man, was reckoned by God to be spiritually dead...What God did is account to them righteousness and spiritual life through their works and obedience...Prior to Jesus coming, men were spiritually dead. God would account to them righteousness for their obedience to the law...If Abraham was spiritually dead, how could God bless him? God could bless him materially because Abraham could act in faith in the material world.'[25] 'Notice also that not one time does God say anything about spiritual blessings, "eternal peace," or anything that could be misconstrued to mean anything other than physical, material blessings.'[26] 'The promises of God to Abraham consisted almost entirely of material prosperity...The only way God could bless man at that time was materially.'[27]

There are so many errors in these quotations that it is obvious that Price does not understand the doctrine of salvation at all. The idea is that the only blessings Abraham received were material ones, because living before the coming of Christ made him ineligible for the spiritual blessings that Christ gave to the church. This is a total misreading of the Bible for Paul shows in *Romans 4* that Abraham was saved in precisely the same way that New Testament believers are saved: 'Abraham believed God, and it was counted unto him for righteousness' *(Romans 4.3)*. Furthermore *Hebrews* tells us that Abraham did not have a mere earthly hope, but looked for a reward in Heaven just as believers do today: 'He looked for a city which hath foundations, whose builder and maker is God' *(Hebrews 11.10)*. He evidently did not regard the earthly blessings given to him by God as the true fulfilment of the covenant promises, for he called himself a stranger and a pilgrim on earth and in doing so showed that he

---

24 Price, *Prosperity: Good News for God's People*, p97
25 Ibid., pp43-45
26 Ibid., p47
27 Ibid., p85

desired 'a better country, that is, an heavenly' *(Hebrews 11.16)*.

Building on his peculiar view of Abraham, Price goes on to teach –

'Paul tells us in *Galatians* that one of the reasons Jesus was cruci-
fied was so that the "blessing of Abraham might come upon *[us]* the
Gentiles".'[28] 'We believers are to receive the promise of the Spirit, and
the blessing of Abraham is supposed to come upon us...the blessing was all physical and material...Now, through Christ Jesus, those
blessings are ours.'[29]

Leroy Thompson also wants us to believe that as the seed of
Abraham, the church has as an inheritance of material blessing: 'the
physical manifestation of prosperity'.[30] Kenneth Copeland inter-
prets the promise of *Deuteronomy 30* as an entirely physical blessing,
including financial benefits.

Contrary to what Price and others teach, the Abrahamic covenant
was essentially a gracious covenant through which Abraham was
saved by faith alone without works, just as believers are today. There
can only be one way of salvation and it is the same in all ages.

There were two parts to the Abrahamic covenant, for it contained
distinct blessings to Abraham's physical seed and to his spiritual
seed. The physical seed were those who were physically descended
from Abraham, Jews by birth, who had the covenant of circumcision
in the flesh. These physical descendants received physical promises – principally, the land of Canaan *(Deuteronomy 8.7-9)*. To Israel
as a nation promises were therefore expressed in material terms,
made to all of them as long as they kept the outward conditions of
the covenant. God would fight for them and deliver their enemies
into their hands; he would give them the rain on their land in due
season *(Deuteronomy 11.14)*, and bless all the work of their hands
so that they could lend to many nations and not need to borrow
(Deuteronomy 28.12).

---

28 Ibid., pp42-43
29 Ibid., p93
30 Thompson, *Money Cometh!* p196

But Abraham also had a spiritual seed, all those people who also walked in the footsteps of Abraham's faith, people of faith who were circumcised not only in their flesh but in their hearts. Through the Abrahamic covenant, promises which were entirely spiritual in nature were given to believing Jews and also to believing Gentiles. Strictly speaking these spiritual promises were made to Abraham's singular Seed, which as Paul explains is Jesus Christ *(Galatians 3.16)*; Abraham and all believers are blessed because they are 'in Christ' and therefore included in the covenant of grace. Just as Abraham saw the physical blessings, such as the land of Canaan, as merely a picture of the true inheritance of God's people, and looked forward to a city not built with hands, so Christians today should see the material promises of the Abrahamic covenant as pictures of the blessings reserved for them in Heaven.

What then are Prosperity Gospel teachers doing? They are taking the earthly, material promises that were given to the physical members of the covenant for their time, and applying them to the spiritual seed. Quite clearly, there are no land promises for Gentile believers today, nor are there those promises that went with the land – protection from national enemies and material prosperity. Abraham was given these and yet, *Hebrews* tells us, he did not set great value on these physical blessings but saw in them God's pledge to give something far more wonderful.

Price insists that the blessings promised to Israel in *Deuteronomy 28* belong to the church, and comments –

> 'There is only one way you can possibly misunderstand this, and that is to somehow claim that the new covenant supersedes, but is not as good as, the old covenant.'[31]

But by what measure are heavenly blessings inferior to material ones? Leroy Thompson protests –

> 'I don't know why it is that, while most of God's people in the Old

---

31 Price, *Prosperity: Good News for God's People*, p95

Testament were rich, most Christians today seem to be broke! We read that we have a better covenant than they had, established upon better promises.'[32]

What state have believers got into when they are unable to value heavenly riches more than earthly, or when they regard the new covenant as deficient unless it includes the material benefits of the old?

Christians do not say, 'The Abrahamic covenant has no relevance for me today so I will ignore it.' Instead, following the guidance of *Hebrews 11*, they translate the language of the Old Testament material blessings into the terms of the new covenant. They see in the land promise a picture of Heaven, and similarly, they see in the Old Testament battles with physical enemies a picture of battles with spiritual enemies. They understand the pillar of cloud and fire that accompanied Israel through the wilderness as evidence that Christ is with them, and the provision of manna, and water from the rock, as God's promise to provide for them. They also take the material wealth promised to Israel as a picture of wealth in the world to come, concerning which 'eye hath not seen, nor ear heard, neither have entered into the heart of man', but 'which God hath prepared for them that love him' *(1 Corinthians 2.9)* – things which far transcend earthly riches.

The effect of prosperity teaching is that these teachers become blind to the spiritual meaning of Scripture. Leroy Thompson quotes *Genesis* – 'God told Abraham, "I'll bless you and I'll make you a blessing" *(Genesis 12.2)*.'[33] But all he can see in these words is a reference to money and wealth. To him, the covenant serves an entirely carnal purpose: 'You see, you need money! And God has provided a covenant whereby you can have it!'[34]

3 John 2 reads, 'Beloved, I wish above all things that thou mayest

---

32 Thompson, *Money Cometh!* p84
33 Ibid., p181
34 Ibid., p183

prosper and be in health, even as thy soul prospereth.' Prosperity teachers make much of this verse because it is the only verse in the New Testament which seems to directly encourage prosperity. They do not seem to know that the Greek word translated 'prosper' means literally 'to lead on a good path'. In the Greek translation of the Old Testament it was used to mean 'to bring to a good conclusion' or 'to succeed'. It occurs in three verses in the New Testament. Firstly in *Romans 1.10* – 'Making request, if by any means now at length I might have a prosperous journey by the will of God to come unto you'. No one would imagine that the apostle was referring to making money.

Secondly, in *1 Corinthians 16.2* – 'Let every one of you lay by him in store, as God hath prospered him.' Here it obviously refers to success in saving for the weekly offering, not to making a profit or becoming rich. The third reference is in *3 John 2* where it clearly refers to all aspects of life, aside from spiritual progress and bodily health mentioned separately. This would include Gaius prospering in good works; in showing hospitality, in help given to needy believers, in family blessings, in friendships, and in many other matters that concerned him. Gaius may need funds to do some of these things and he could certainly ask God to provide, but it does not fit the passage for John to limit his concern to the matter of financial enrichment. What delights John is not to hear that Gaius is made rich, but that he is walking in the truth. This man was certainly wealthier than most believers in the church for he was able to entertain visiting teachers sent from John, but such behaviour is quite consistent with a modest lifestyle.

6 – Promoting wants over needs

Although the promises given to national, physical Israel have not been transported wholesale into the new covenant, there are assurances from God concerning our physical state in this world. Believers are right to trust the Lord for their bodily as well as their spiritual needs. But none of the promises in the New Testament about our physical needs entitle us to ask for riches. Scripture gives a strong warning against such an attitude, saying – 'But they that will be rich fall into temptation and a snare, and into many foolish and hurtful lusts, which drown men in destruction and perdition' *(1 Timothy 6.9)*.

We may confidently come to the Lord and pray, 'Give us this day our daily bread,' but we may not ask, 'Lord, give me the car I want; give me the house I want; fill my bank account so that I don't have to worry about my earthly needs and so that I have physical security.' God will do nothing to inflame our lusts. Note that we are only authorised to ask for the basic necessities by the Lord's Prayer – bread. Another picture of what the Lord provides is seen in the supply of manna in the wilderness which was sufficient for the present day but could not be stored up for the next.

We have a very specific promise of provision given to us by Paul, 'But my God shall supply all your need according to his riches in glory by Christ Jesus' *(Philippians 4.19)*, but again, notice that it is *our needs* not *our wants* that are supplied, a distinction conveniently ignored by the prosperity teachers. The idea that God wants all his people to be prosperous and suffer no lack at all is not supported by Scripture. John the Baptist taught, 'He that hath two coats, let him impart to him that hath none; and he that hath meat, let him do likewise' *(Luke 3.11)*. Having only two coats, giving one away and being left with one, is hardly a picture of the affluence that prosperity teachers advocate.

Furthermore, prosperity teachers exaggerate the provision that Old Testament saints received from God. Jacob expressed his thanks to 'the God which fed me all my life long unto this day' *(Genesis 48.15)*. But that provision included Jacob's long period of servitude in Syria to Laban, as well as two instances of severe famine which necessitated his sons being dispatched to Egypt to buy bread. God did prosper his people Israel when they were obedient to him, but there were still limits set in the area of possessions, and acquisitiveness was never their great goal. Moses, inspired by God, set a standard for any king that would arise in the future: 'He shall not multiply horses to himself...neither shall he multiply wives to himself, that his heart turn not away: neither shall he greatly multiply to himself silver and gold' *(Deuteronomy 17.16-17)*.

Does God ever give wealth to his people? He does, but not by their design. God is sovereign in this matter. Certainly there were rich men in the New Testament as well as in the Old Testament, but these were exceptional within the church, and must not be made the pattern to which all should aspire.

7 – Ignoring the sin of covetousness

In contrast to the very modest requests for earthly needs that we find God's people encouraged to make in Scripture, the Prosperity Gospel advocates something shockingly different. Any illusion that prosperity teachers are simply trying to deliver Christians from poverty and help them to pay off their debts is soon dispelled when we read some of the extreme statements that they make about wealth. The reader is struck by the irresponsible nature of their incitements to gain wealth, and soon sees that this is not remotely like the outlook taught in Scripture.

First, these teachers want to put financial matters high on the believer's agenda. T. D. Jakes tells us, 'Joseph had a plan. Many people fail to attain their financial goals because they have no plan.'[35] He then proceeds to make Joseph's actions as governor of Egypt a model for how Christians should handle their financial affairs. But their manner of handling the Scripture is an example of twisting it to one's own destruction.

Creflo Dollar encourages his hearers to enjoy riches early in life –

'The world's system...teaches you to put away money while you're

---

35 Jakes, *The Great Investment*, p70

young so that you can become wealthy when you are old. Although that sounds reasonable, and I certainly believe in saving money, I think most of us would prefer to be millionaires at thirty, forty, fifty, and sixty.'[36]

Get all you can in this world is Leroy Thompson's advice:

'If you don't already live in Florida, wouldn't it be wonderful to have a nice house there so that when it gets cold, you could "fly away" from the cold weather and sit on a beach somewhere? You could call back home to your state and ask your friends how they are doing back there. You could tell them, "I'm on vacation. I'll be back in three weeks!" Some people get "holy" on you when you talk like that, and they look at you like you're strange. But, you see, that's what God expects for you! If anybody is supposed to be out there on the beach sucking pineapple juice with a soft straw, it ought to be us [Christians]!'[37]

It is nothing to this man to be using his wealth for personal gratification, and boasting of his riches to his friends. He continues –

'I want to help you cleanse your mind because if you have a religious mindset, you're not going to hear what I'm saying...Suppose for a moment that you were a multimillionaire businessman, and your 25 year old son just found the girl of his dreams and married her...Your son sees a house that he really likes. You need to spend some money because of taxes; you've got too much money! The house your son likes costs no more than $175,000...So you say to your sweet little daughter-in-law, "Do you like that house, Honey?" She says, "Yes." So you say, "Then call the realtor. Tell him you want it, and tell him I'm financing it. It's paid for in full. I'm going to pay for the furniture too!"...I'm trying to change your thinking – to raise your level of thinking.'[38]

Christians are to think of God like this indulgent millionaire father. In making requests to him, there are to be no questions asked, no thought of the consequences of indulging our every material whim, no consideration of what is the will of God, or what is wise, no fear of spoiling the believer.

---

36 Dr Creflo Dollar, *The Holy Spirit, Your Financial Advisor*, p122, Faith Words, 2013
37 Thompson, *Money Cometh!* p14
38 Ibid., pp15-16

Commenting on the changes in his own lifestyle, Thompson says –

'I never used to fly first class. God had to really work with me...The Spirit of God once said to me, "Why do you keep passing up those first-class seats? When are you going to have faith for those seats?"...One time...The airline bumped me up to first class...Another time, I ended up in first class again...After that, I made up my mind that God is a first-class God and from that day forward, I began to fly first class!...So I fly first class now and I'm not bothered by it at all.'[39]

This behaviour is in stark contrast to Lord Radstock, the English peer, whose evangelistic efforts among the nobility of Russia revitalised the evangelical church in that land at a time when it was near to being smothered by the deadening influence of the Russian Orthodox Church. It is recorded that, 'on one occasion, going by train, when he was using third class travel, somebody said to him, "Why do you travel third class?" He said, "Because there's no fourth class."'[40] He understood that Christians are called to live frugal, simple lifestyles, not to be 'in it for all they can get'.

Thompson quotes *Psalm 34* – 'They that seek the Lord shall not want any good thing.' He asks –

'Is it a good thing to have all your bills paid? Is it a good thing to eat the kind of steak or food you like?...Is it a good thing to have a nice car to go where you want to go with your family and get back safely?...Is having a nice, new outfit a good thing?...If I walked into a house and saw five turkeys on the table with their legs stuck up in the air, I'd say, "the Lord is in this house. This is a blessed house!"'[41]

If we measure life by a fleshly, finite perspective then we will reckon that anything that improves our earthly lot is a good thing, but the Christian does not see his life like this. He knows he cannot walk by sight, but that life is a training ground and the reason he is left in this world is to prepare him for eternity, not to make him super-comfortable here. If God in his wisdom allows us to go through a

39 Thompson, *Money Cometh!* p241
40 David Fountain, *Lord Radstock and the Russian Awakening*, p54, Mayflower Christian Books, 1988
41 Thompson, *Money Cometh!* pp264, 267

period of scarcity then the believer accepts this; for he has the long view in mind and trusts the providence of God to lead him by the best path. By faith, he does not complain if things get hard.

Thompson defines prosperity for us –

'What does "rich" mean? "Rich" doesn't mean you have $5,000,000 in the bank. But it does mean that all your bills are paid and you are out of debt. It means driving the kind of car you want. It means having the kind of house you want ... God is not holding houses or cars back from you ... As a matter of fact, He'd rather you live in a big house. He would rather you drive a big car or the kind of car you want. ... Some people say, "It's not spiritual to talk about houses and cars." But those same people will do everything they can, spiritual or not, to have a better house or a better car and to do nicely in life! Why else would they be working so hard on the job?' [42]

This analysis of believers – presumably he is talking about believers – comes close to the devil's cynical analysis of Job's motivation: 'Doth Job fear God for nought?' *(Job 1.9)*. How is it that this writer can see no other reason why Christians work hard at what they do than to get the biggest car and the biggest house they can?

John Avanzini also wants to raise the fleshly expectations of believers. Referring to the parable of the sower – 'he shall receive an hundredfold now in this time' – he comments –

'Imagine getting back thirty dollars for giving a dollar, six thousand dollars for giving a hundred, a hundred thousand dollars or more for giving a thousand. This rate of return sounds impossible to most folks. Well it didn't seem the least bit impossible to Jesus. In fact, he actually taught these outrageous rates of increase. If you will read this material with an open mind and faithfully put its principles to work, you will be able to manifest these same increases in your own finances.'[43]

What poverty, spiritually speaking, belongs to those congregations that have to rely on this sort of exposition of God's Word! The Gospel delivers people out of a mindset that sees everything in terms

---

42 Ibid., p213
43 John Avanzini, *What Jesus Taught About Manifesting Abundance*, p9, Harrison House, 1996

of material gain and personal advance, but the Prosperity Gospel throws people right back into it again.

What about the danger of covetousness in all the encouragement to acquire and enjoy earthly riches? These teachers are not unaware of the problem and at times they will issue warnings. One way that they try to deal with the issue is to imagine there is a difference between the way the world seeks wealth and the way the Christian does so. Price explains –

> 'The world's system focuses on the material and the physical. It tells you there is no God, and there is only what you make out of life. God's prosperity system requires that you start with the spiritual, and it will eventually be revealed in this material world.'[44]

The trouble with this piece of self-deception is that it sidesteps the clear warnings that God gives that we should never pursue personal wealth. Prosperity teachers tell us that we can safely accumulate riches in this world as long as we put God first. In other words, these teachers claim that you can serve both God and mammon without falling. But we have seen the fruit of this overconfidence in the scandalous downfalls of those who have advocated this way of life. Their over-indulgence has often been brought to public attention following their moral collapse, and God's people have wondered how they could ever have justified these excesses to themselves. It started with reasoning such as that given above by Price.

He turns to the encounter of Christ with the rich young ruler to claim that there is nothing more to covetousness than fear – a fear of losing what we possess. He therefore believes that once we replace this fear by faith, wealth holds no danger for us. The rich young ruler, he suggests, was obsessed with this fear and so could not sell his goods. While fear of losing earthly security may be one element of covetousness, there is more to it than that. Paul teaches that 'covetousness ... is idolatry' *(Colossians 3.5)*, and therefore there is a

---

44 Price, *Prosperity: Good News for God's People*, pp114-115

love of money in the heart of the covetous man. It is always danger-
ous to pursue prosperity since it forms an idolatrous substitute for
God as soon as we love it.

T. D. Jakes makes a more serious attempt to warn of danger when
he says –

> 'There are others who get caught up in the material world and equate
> wealth with strength of faith. They believe that God's blessings can
> be counted in dollars and cents, and one's financial status is an indi-
> cation of one's status in the eyes of the Lord. They begin pursuing
> money for money's sake. Material goods become their gods, and
> banks become their churches. They lose sight of the fact that although
> God does indeed bless us with financial success, we should be mindful
> to worship the Giver and not the gift.'[45]

The trouble with this warning is that he does not see that it is
impossible for someone to desire to be rich without falling 'into
temptation and a snare, and into many foolish and hurtful lusts,
which drown men in destruction and perdition' *(1 Timothy 6.9)*.
He wants to take account of this text, and yet he also wants to urge
people to pursue prosperity. We are being given conflicting advice,
and many will respond to this as Balaam did. Peter tells us that this
false prophet 'loved the wages of unrighteousness' *(2 Peter 2.15)*. The
warnings of the prosperity teachers have a hollow ring.

Another example of a man who was ruined by the love of riches is
Gehazi, Elisha's servant. He could not bear the thought of his master
passing up the opportunity to receive a handsome financial reward
from Naaman for healing him of his leprosy, for he knew that Elisha
had declined any gift. He therefore went secretly back to Naaman
and lied in order to get what he wanted. Elisha's searching question to him was this: 'Is it a time to receive money, and to receive
garments, and oliveyards, and vineyards, and sheep, and oxen, and
menservants, and maidservants?' *(2 Kings 5.26)*. Gehazi was a covetous man and deception naturally attached itself to his covetousness.

---

45 Jakes, *The Great Investment*, p4

He saw godliness as a means to an end – his own personal enrichment. Why are prosperity teachers not trembling at the thought that they have fallen into the same trap as Gehazi?

How do these teachers dare to abandon the carefully worded instruction of Scripture on this subject and strike such a different note? We could look at many places in Scripture where warnings are given against covetousness, but we mention just a few by way of example. The qualification for the judges who were to assist Moses was they should be 'men of truth, hating covetousness' *(Exodus 18.21)*. Similarly Paul says that elders in the churches should be 'not covetous' *(1 Timothy 3.3)*; Jeremiah berates the leaders of Israel because, 'every one from the least even unto the greatest is given to covetousness, from the prophet even unto the priest every one dealeth falsely' *(Jeremiah 8.10)*.

David prays, 'Incline my heart unto thy testimonies, and not to covetousness' *(Psalm 119.36)*. The writer of *Proverbs 30.8-9* prays, 'Remove far from me vanity and lies: give me neither poverty nor riches; feed me with food convenient for me: lest I be full, and deny thee, and say, Who is the Lord? or lest I be poor, and steal, and take the name of my God in vain.' Solomon, because he knew the weakness of his own heart, is commended by God. He had not asked for riches but for wisdom *(2 Chronicles 1.10)*. But why should we not pray for riches if the prosperity writers are correct that God's will is that all his people become wealthy?

Paul tells us that when he came to Thessalonica he did not use 'a cloak of covetousness' *(1 Thessalonians 2.5)*. The expression is very instructive because it shows that covetousness often goes hand in hand with deception. The expression pictures covetousness being covered and hidden by a cloak of concern for human souls; Paul denies that he operated in this way.

Peter describes a type of teacher who will plague the people of God in the last times – 'But there were false prophets also among the people, even as there shall be false teachers among you, who privily shall bring in damnable heresies, even denying the Lord that bought them, and bring upon themselves swift destruction. And many shall follow their pernicious ways; by reason of whom the way of truth shall be evil spoken of. And through covetousness shall they with feigned words make merchandise of you: whose judgment now of a long time lingereth not, and their damnation slumbereth not' *(2 Peter 2.1-3).*

Are we not seeing a fulfilment of this prophecy today in the Prosperity Gospel and the Word of Faith movement, for this passage so accurately describes what we see happening among them. Covetousness is at the heart of what is wrong with their message, as they exploit covetousness while making a pretence of wanting to benefit the people of God. All the while, they are making merchandise out of God's people for they successfully syphon off large slices of the profits for themselves, as is evident from the outrageously affluent lifestyles many of them live. Furthermore, they bring the Gospel into disrepute by setting up an easy target for those who wish to dismiss the church as a self-seeking institution, feigning a desire to care for people's spiritual needs.

These writers are also capable of alarming throw-away remarks that reveal a culture within their churches where there is little sense of shame over covetousness or other evils that follow from it. Thompson admits –

'Now I didn't have any money back then, but I always had a front. In other words, I always had a new car, but I was just as broke as I could be ... Everybody you see driving a new car isn't rich. He may be broke, trying to pay for that car! That's the way it was in my case.'[46] 'I acted like I was rich all the time even when I was broke.'[47]

An appearance of wealth was so important to him that he was prepared to put on a charade of being financially blessed.

Thompson remarks that some poverty is self-induced –

---

46 Thompson, *Money Cometh!* p60
47 Ibid., p153

'Some Christians bring sorrow upon themselves financially by getting caught up in gambling casinos, spinning those wheels and trying to get rich. But why are all those Christians in those places spinning those wheels when the Father has provided a sure thing for them?... That's why a lot of those Christians gamble; not necessarily because they are bad Christians, but because they're broke. They want to hit the jackpot and have some money.'[48]

Benny Hinn unguardedly reports –

'Each week fully two-thirds of the calls and letters we receive request prayer for financial breakthrough. Think of it – thousands upon thousands of people each and every week request prayer for financial needs alone.'[49]

Thompson indicates the inability of those in his circle to live without prosperity, when he describes a family among his congregation in reduced circumstances. His comments show the strain that covetousness puts on relationships –

'Being broke has caused more fussing and fighting among husbands and wives than just about anything.'[50] 'There's not much glory in going home to a distressed and discontented husband or wife and hearing a bunch of nagging because you're always broke.'[51]

It is not so much poverty as covetousness which is the root of the problem here. God's solution is not necessarily to supply us with the wealth which we lack, but to teach us to appreciate the far greater spiritual riches which every one of his children already possesses. He may bring us out of difficult circumstances, but there may be lessons which we need to learn while we are still in them. The Scripture says, 'Let your conversation be without covetousness; and be content with such things as ye have: for he hath said, I will never leave thee, nor forsake thee' (Hebrews 13.5).

When one man came to Christ and said, 'Master, speak to my

---

48 Thompson, *Money Cometh!* pp293-294
49 Benny Hinn, *The Biblical Road to Blessing*, p9, Thomas Nelson, 1997
50 Thompson, *Money Cometh!* p30
51 Ibid., p277

brother, that he divide the inheritance with me,' the Lord answered him, 'Man, who made me a judge or a divider over you?' and said to his disciples afterwards, 'Take heed, and beware of covetousness: for a man's life consisteth not in the abundance of the things which he possesseth' *(Luke 12.13-15)*.

God commands his people not to love this present world *(1 John 2.15-16)*. Scripture views the world as a spiritual kingdom at war with God and his people. We are born as those who belong to the world and have the world within us. At conversion Christ delivers us out of the world, releasing us from an obligation to serve it, and he takes the world from our hearts and causes us to see that God is our highest good, and our happiness comes alone from him. From that moment on the devil strives to reassert his rights over us, and to get us to return to our old way of life and thinking. The Christian has to resist this pressure and to keep the world from re-entering his heart. This is why the Prosperity Gospel does so much damage, for it teaches God's people that the things of the world are both desirable and manageable. Christians can safely allow a love for the here and now to enter back into them, and can lust after better and bigger cars and houses, and other possessions. They can support the work of the Gospel, and at the same time cut off a generous slice of this world's cake for themselves. But God is jealous for his people and he knows how quickly their love for him grows cold when they start to appreciate their possessions too much. It is not only trust in riches that is condemned, but also loving them too much, and deriving too much pleasure from them.

The tenth commandment states, 'Thou shalt not covet thy neighbour's house, thou shalt not covet thy neighbour's wife, nor his manservant, nor his maidservant, nor his ox, nor his ass, nor any thing that is thy neighbour's' *(Exodus 20.17)*. What is forbidden by this commandment is making an idol out of any created thing so that it rivals God in our hearts, and becomes something which we live for and cannot be happy without. Covetousness shows itself not only when we love and serve the things of this world too much, but also when we fall into misery and jealousy of others because we do not have what they have. It was through this commandment that the apostle Paul tells us he became aware of his sin as the Spirit of God revealed to him the covetousness of his own heart. He saw that however much he appeared to be a righteous Pharisee on the outside, on the inside he harboured an uncontrolled lust, and this knowledge of himself brought him to the point where he despaired of ever successfully keeping God's commandment. He felt the law's sentence of death within him. But the prosperity teachers have taken away the tenth commandment by teaching that it is no sin to desire to be rich, so that they undermine the commandment and prevent the law doing its work of conviction. They pretend that they still warn against the danger of covetousness, but at the same time they encourage a desire to be rich which is at the heart of this sin. How many souls, we wonder, have been denied the possibility of being brought under conviction of sin by this deceitful teaching!

8 – Evangelising by trust in money

One major argument prosperity writers use for justifying the seeking of wealth is that without money the world cannot be evangelised. Evangelism is an expensive business, they claim, and the world cannot be reached without God's people pouring their wealth into the work. Kenneth Copeland reports God's message to him –

> 'When I was in Africa, the Lord told me that He is holding the body of Christ in every nation responsible for winning their own lost. It takes money to finance a revival.'[52]

Similarly Frederick Price says –

> 'More than ever, the body of Christ needs money to spread the Gospel. Even the simplest Bible tracts cost money; but getting the attention of people in the twenty-first century – including those in so-called Third World countries – demands much more than simple

---

52 Copeland, *Prosperity: The Choice is Yours*, p9

tracts . . . sophisticated, yet personal, methods of spreading the good news of Jesus Christ are more necessary than ever. Television costs money. Satellite communication costs money. Email programs and websites cost money. Airplanes that can carry you to the uttermost parts of the earth cost money. God knew this from the beginning. He knew that Christians would need money in this age to compete with the secular media . . . From the devil's perspective, when you see a wealthy Christian, you see someone who is a tremendous threat to his agenda. That is a person who can leverage money for the kingdom in ways that poor Christians cannot.'[53]

T. D. Jakes asks –

'How much more impact these good Christians could have had if only they availed themselves of the riches the world offered.'[54]

Creflo Dollar bemoans the situation –

'I could make millions of dollars a year, and it still wouldn't be enough to pay for the television programming needed to reach the millions of people who have not yet heard the Gospel . . . Therefore, it is vital that we begin to see money as a means to an end. In other words, money is a tool God can use to further the Gospel.'[55]

Leroy Thompson tells us how God works –

'The Lord is going to finance the propagation of His Gospel throughout the earth, and He wants to use some of your money to do it! . . . God wants us to have money so we can spread the Gospel and bring Bibles to those who have never heard about Jesus . . . We need to build churches and send ministers out to preach the Gospel. We need millions of dollars to do that, and God is giving it to us!'[56]

Without money, some souls will be lost –

'Many souls will miss the Kingdom of God because some in the Body of Christ lived below their rights and privileges. I am convinced that some will not enter the Kingdom because the Body of Christ missed the part of the Gospel that would have brought them into the prosperity that God provided through His promise to Father Abraham and through the Lord Jesus Christ . . . But when the church has a poverty

53 Price, *Prosperity: Good News for God's People*, pp5-7
54 Jakes, *The Great Investment*, p15
55 Dollar, *The Holy Spirit, Your Financial Advisor*, p125
56 Thompson, *Money Cometh!* pp8, 21

mentality, the Gospel can't go forth as God wants it to go forth.'[57]

In opposition to all this teaching, Zechariah sums up the means God uses to win the lost, 'Not by might, nor by power, but by my spirit, saith the Lord of hosts' *(Zechariah 4.6)*. It is not by human wealth that the kingdom of Heaven advances, because it is a spiritual kingdom which only makes gains through the operation of spiritual means. God will ensure that he gets himself the glory for the advance of his own cause, and will not allow the credit to go to any carnal means. God teaches us through the physical battles which Israel fought long ago – the thirty-two thousand with Gideon were whittled down to three hundred men to be sent against the Midianites, 'lest Israel vaunt themselves against me, saying, Mine own hand hath saved me' *(Judges 7.2)*. So also Asa, in facing a vastly greater army than his own, prayed, 'Lord, it is nothing with thee to help, whether with many, or with them that have no power: help us, O Lord our God; for we rest on thee, and in thy name we go against this multitude' *(2 Chronicles 14.11)*.

The disciples of Christ were sent out without great material resources, just because they had to live by the Gospel in reliance upon the Lord's provision and not on the arm of flesh. The work of winning souls is a spiritual work which cannot succeed without dependence on the Spirit of God who alone can convert sinners, and a readiness to work according to God's revealed methods. His primary means of winning the lost is preaching: through proclamation of the message of the Gospel as revealed in Scripture. The soul-winner must be willing to pay, especially in terms of courage, labour, conviction, and compassion. The kingdom of Heaven advances through faith, such as that displayed by David in defeating Goliath single-handed, or by Jonathan in raiding the Philistine garrison with only his armour-bearer to help.

Great victories have been won for Christ in the past through

57 Thompson, *Money Cometh!* pp196-197

those who were willing to lay down their lives for the Gospel. Paul summarises his apostolic calling, a life dedicated to the winning of the lost: 'In labours more abundant, in stripes above measure, in prisons more frequent, in deaths oft. Of the Jews five times received I forty stripes save one. Thrice was I beaten with rods, once was I stoned, thrice I suffered shipwreck, a night and a day I have been in the deep; in journeyings often, in perils of waters, in perils of robbers, in perils by mine own countrymen, in perils by the heathen, in perils in the city, in perils in the wilderness, in perils in the sea, in perils among false brethren; in weariness and painfulness, in watchings often, in hunger and thirst, in fastings often, in cold and nakedness' *(2 Corinthians 11.23-27)*.

All these things the apostle Paul was willing to pay in order to reach the lost. God will not permit material wealth to take over and take the credit for the evangelisation of the world, 'that no flesh should glory in his presence' *(1 Corinthians 1.29)*. He will not use and bless the carnal, money-dependent evangelism of the prosperity teachers.

Does this mean that Christians should not assist with expensive schemes to win the lost when good opportunities present themselves? Not at all! We may pay for the translation, printing and distribution of books, we may support Christian workers in our own land and overseas, and we may pay for websites and television broadcasts to take the Gospel to people, and we test all these things to see what methods they use and what message they bring. God has ordained preaching as the primary means by which the lost are won.

Usually Prosperity Gospel teachers persuade people to give for evangelism in order that they may be rewarded by God and given more in return. That is a terrible motive for evangelism and for giving. It is selfish and fleshly, and God would surely never bless such stewardship for self-enrichment. When Saul allowed the people to keep the spoil of the Amalekites which he had been commanded to destroy, he sinfully excused himself by saying that he intended to use this spoil to offer sacrifices to the Lord *(1 Samuel 15.20-22)*.

Prosperity teachers collect money supposedly for evangelism, then keep much of it for their excessive lifestyles.

In any case, what sort of Gospel do these prosperity teachers wish to finance? If it is a gospel of prosperity, it would be far better if it were never even heard among men. Kenneth Copeland believes that he has a new message to preach – the gospel to the poor. According to him, Christ's words have never yet been fulfilled when he said, 'The Spirit of the Lord is upon me, because he hath anointed me to preach the gospel to the poor' *(Luke 4.18)*. Copeland tells us –

> 'The gospel to the poor is that Jesus has come and they don't have to be poor anymore! Not very many poverty-stricken people have ever heard the whole gospel.'[58]

He asks –

> 'How can they believe for any prosperity in Africa or India, where drought and famine have become a way of life?'[59]

The phrase 'believe for any prosperity' should be noted. He means that they should not believe just for salvation but for prosperity as well, because prosperity is supposedly part of the Gospel. In his mind the preaching of the Gospel is connected with the elimination of poverty, but this is contrary to the Bible where the Gospel is defined very clearly for us; it is 'that Christ died for our sins according to the scriptures; and that he was buried, and that he rose again the third day according to the scriptures' *(1 Corinthians 15.3-4)*. However concerned Christians may be to alleviate need in the world, it is not promised as part of Gospel preaching, and will not be eliminated while this world lasts, for 'ye have the poor with you always' *(Mark 14.7)*.

9 – Replacing faith by will-power

The Word of Faith movement makes *the power to acquire* a major theme in its teaching. The name 'Word of Faith' adopted by the

---

58 Copeland, *Prosperity: The Choice is Yours*, p9
59 Ibid., p9

movement comes from *Romans 10.8* – 'The word is nigh thee, even in thy mouth, and in thy heart: that is, the word of faith, which we preach.' However, the 'word of faith' is defined as a power possessed by believers to use words spoken in faith as a creative force, bringing into existence things that they think God has already promised, and which he will make a reality as the power of faith is exercised. This involves speaking out loud words which lay claim to the blessings of God, particularly in the area of health and wealth. It is called 'positive confession' and is contrasted with negative confession which is seen when people focus on fears which they should not fall prey to. Teachers of this practice cite Job as an example of negative confession, when he stated, 'For the thing which I greatly feared is come upon me' *(Job 3.25)*, thereby supposedly bringing his sufferings upon himself. Price says –

> 'Job was a man afraid. He was not walking in complete faith...Job was afraid that his sons (and daughters) were sinning...I never once worried that any of my three daughters or my son had cursed God in their hearts.'[60]

Allowing fears to come into the mind and take hold of our thinking is said to be harmful and is why prosperity teachers encourage their readers to reinforce 'positive' attitudes in their minds. Creflo Dollar gives a list of prosperity mantras to be repeated by the believer over and over again until he is unable to doubt what he tells himself. Among these are the following,

> '*Psalm 35.27* says God delights in the prosperity of His servants. Therefore, as His servant, I declare that I am out of debt, my needs are met, and I have plenty more to put in store.'[61]

> 'God delights in my prosperity. He gives me power to get wealth so that He may establish His covenant upon the earth *(Deuteronomy 8.18)*.'[62]

---

60 Price, *Prosperity: Good News for God's People*, p117
61 Dollar, *The Holy Spirit, Your Financial Advisor*, p92
62 Ibid., p93

'I renew my mind to the truth about God's desire to financially prosper me.'[63]

Dollar wants to get us to think in a new way –

'Many people are living below the standard that God desires for them, and they can't break free because of the way they think. As a result, they have positioned themselves for failure...It is critical that we recognise the poverty mindset and break out of it by applying and practising God's word concerning prosperity.'[64]

Thompson is particularly strong on self-programming –

'If you're in the Body of Christ, say this out loud: "Money cometh to the Body of Christ! That means money cometh to me now! God wants me to have plenty of money so I can carry out his covenant." '[65] "Say this out loud: "God wants me to be blessed. As matter of fact, I am blessed. From now on, I'll speak words of prosperity. I won't speak against prosperity." ' [66]

Kenneth Copeland urges Christians to see themselves as providing a blessing to the world –

'Change your image today. Begin seeing yourself as the one giving to supply the needs of mankind ... Walk in that revelation today! You are a giver.'[67]

Belief in the power of 'confession' is based partly on the extraordinary idea that God himself has faith and exercised faith in the creation of the world and that Christians are to imitate God's faith. E. W. Kenyon stated –

'Faith is the creative force in man. Faith is the creative force in the Creator. God simply said, "Let there be." '[68]

Kenneth Hagin added –

'The God kind of faith is the kind of faith that spoke the world into

63 Dollar, *The Holy Spirit, Your Financial Advisor*, p93
64 Ibid., p99
65 Thompson, *Money Cometh!* p9
66 Ibid., p33
67 Copeland, *Prosperity: The Choice is Yours*, p38
68 E. W. Kenyon, *Two Kinds of Knowledge*, pp14-15, Kenyon Gospel Publishers, 1981

existence...God created the universe with words. Words filled with faith are the most powerful things in all the world.'[69]

Kenneth Copeland supports this idea –

'The world and the physical forces governing it were created by the power of faith – a spiritual force. God, a Spirit, created all matter and he created it with the force of faith.'[70]

But God does not exercise faith, because faith involves dependence on and trust in another. The one who needs to exercise faith has imperfect knowledge and power, and needs to believe in someone else who knows the way or has the power to do something. God is the source of all knowledge and power, and is all-sufficient in himself. He knows all things and is dependent on no one, and therefore has no need to exercise faith. The notion that we are to imitate God's faith shows great ignorance of the Bible and of the doctrine of God.

Prosperity Gospel teachers quote *Mark 11.22* to justify their unorthodox idea. 'And Jesus answering saith unto them, Have faith in God.' They very strangely interpret this to mean, 'Have the kind of faith God has', as though the words of Christ refer to God's faith, rather than our faith in him. (It should be obvious to them that the context of the passage is Christ teaching his disciples to pray, and it is their faith that is in mind, not God's.)

They also claim that *Hebrews 11.3* supports their idea: 'Through faith we understand that the worlds were framed by the word of God.' They take this to mean that God created the world by speaking words of faith. Price argues that *Hebrews 11.3* –

'is not just saying that by an exercise of our faith we believe that God spoke the world into existence. It is saying that, but it's also saying much more. It's telling us how God did it! By using his faith!'[71]

---

69 Kenneth E. Hagin, *New Thresholds of Faith*, pp74-76, Kenneth Hagin Ministries, 1989

70 Kenneth Copeland, *The Laws of Prosperity*, pp18-19, Kenneth Copeland Publications, 1974

71 Frederick K. C. Price, *How Faith Works*, pp99, 101, Harrison House, 1976

Price wants to have it both ways: 'the believer knows this by faith,' and 'the believer knows that God did it by faith,' but the sentence cannot mean both things at once. (The words 'by faith' and 'by the word of God' are separated in the original Greek, preventing them being linked together. Teachers like Price do not seem to know this.) The verse is clearly in harmony with the surrounding verses which all refer to the faith of God's people, not to God's faith.

We are never told in the Bible that our words have creative power, even in minor matters, or that they possess the power to bring positive benefits into our lives. We are to present our needs before God, ask him for our daily bread, and live in dependence on him. We are to ask even though he knows our needs before we ask. It is he who provides for us, and he insists that we come to him constantly with our requests and acknowledge him as our provider. Scripture never teaches that prayer can be dispensed with on the basis that God has already given us things, and we should simply claim these things by faith.

It is a vital principle not understood by prosperity teachers that faith is not entitled to believe anything beyond what God has revealed in his Word. We cannot simply invent matters to believe in, and then claim that because we exercise faith God is obliged to give us what we ask, and to bring whatever we visualise into existence. Faith must have an authority for what it believes, and that authority is God's Word. When Christ wanted those on the road to Emmaus to overcome their doubts and believe the resurrection, he expounded to them the scriptures on this subject: this was the authority they needed to convince them. The only firm basis for what we believe in matters of religion is what God has revealed in his Word, the Bible, and we must not go beyond this.

In principle, Word of Faith teachers would not disagree with this, but in practice they depart far from it. Not only do they add private revelations of their own, but in teaching about faith, they encourage Christians to make claims on God regarding many things for which they have no direction in Scripture.

It is wrong, according to them, to doubt that God wills every believer to be financially prosperous. But the belief that all Christians should be rich is contrary to the Bible, and the evangelists of the New Testament, led by Paul, were never rich. (We say more on this shortly.) Faith to possess wealth is not commanded or authorised in the New Testament. Faith needs the authority of the Word; only then may it lay hold of God's promises, and ask on the basis of these promises. If and when the blessing comes, it is God who provides, and not faith. It is God who has brought it into being, not faith. The prosperity approach to faith makes it impossible to wait on God, nor does it allow for the possibility that God declines to give us what we ask. Prosperity teachers encourage their followers to be certain that they will receive all that they ask for. Leroy Thompson in a section headed 'Claim Your Benefits Today' says –

> 'There are certain benefits that belong to me and you, as heirs and children of God ... We are not going to receive the inheritance *[in the future]*. We can go ahead and collect our inheritance now!'[72]

Some aspects of the will of God are fully revealed and others are only partially revealed. We may, for example, pray with complete assurance that it is God's will that the Gospel should be preached to every nation, and kindred, and tongue and people, for God has commanded this. In the same way we may pray for personal sanctification because God has commanded us to be holy and there is no doubt that we are saved for this purpose. But other matters are not so clear. We cannot be certain about the specific details of our lives such as where we live, what job we do, or who we should marry. None of these things are revealed in God's Word, and we are warned that it is vain boasting to claim to know more than we do, or to dictate to God what the details of our lives should be. We should always pray for such things, but with humble submission to God's

---

72 Thompson, *Money Cometh!* p212

secret will. Our health definitely falls within this second category of things uncertain, for we must leave it to the wisdom of God whether he grants us good health, or whether he appoints trials for us in the form of sickness, so that 'the trying of *[our]* faith worketh patience' *(James 1.3)*. In the case of wealth however we may pray with scriptural authority for the supply of needs, but not for wealth – for that is in God's unrevealed will.

10 – Inventing wealth for Jesus and his apostles

Another bizarre theme of interest to these teachers is the idea that the Lord Jesus Christ and his disciples were actually rich on earth in terms of material wealth. This is a hard case for them to make, but is necessary in order to defend the Prosperity Gospel from the charge of utter inconsistency. Clearly if the New Testament presents Christ as having a lifestyle markedly different from that advocated by these teachers, it would be a severe embarrassment to them. However, the arguments used do not make the case which they claim to make. It is one thing to prove that Christ and the apostles were not living in abject poverty; it is another to show that they were wealthy to the extent that prosperity teachers believe. While orthodox Christian teachers have never taught that Christ and his disciples lived in a state of poverty on earth, they have seen unmistakable evidence in the New Testament that they lived a simple lifestyle without any of the trappings of wealth and luxury that are so sought after by the Prosperity Gospel movement.

In answer to a remark made to Hagin that 'Jesus and his disciples never drove a Cadillac', he answers with the fatuous comment, 'There weren't any Cadillacs then. But Jesus did ride a donkey. It was the "Cadillac" of that day – the best means of transportation they had.'[73]

Frederick Price uses a number of arguments. We should not read

---

73 Hagin, *The Believer's Authority*, p47

Matthew 8.20 too literally, he tells us, 'Foxes have holes, and the birds of the air have nests, but the Son of man hath not where to lay his head' – for in '*Matthew 13.1*, it says, "On the same day Jesus went *out of the house* and sat by the sea." I doubt that He owned the house,' he comments, 'but obviously He had money to rent.'[74]

Matthew's Gospel tells us that Jesus left Nazareth and made his base in Capernaum *(Matthew 4.13)* and that Peter lived there with his wife and mother-in-law *(Matthew 8.5, 14)*, and Andrew his brother *(Mark 1.29)*. It is far more likely that this was Peter's own house than that Jesus rented it. Peter previously had a fishing business and there is certainly nothing surprising in the fact that he owned his own house.

Price asks what Joseph and Mary would have done with the gifts of the Magi, which he assumes amounted to several boxes of gold coins, and concludes that as trustees for their son they probably invested it in the Nazareth area. From this remark he jumps to the unlikely conclusion –

> 'At the time of His anointing, then, when He went into the water at the Jordan River, Jesus had at least one, but most likely many boxes of gold awaiting Him in Nazareth for His many missionary journeys. He also had the money He Himself earned. Traditionally He is referred to as a carpenter, but back then the term included carpentry and masonry. He was an all-purpose general contractor.'[75]

It would be surprising if any of the Magi's gold remained over to Jesus' adult life, even if this was more than a token amount. Joseph needed money in order to care for his family while they were away from home – he rented a house in Bethlehem for a time – and they would have needed money in order to travel to Egypt and live there while fleeing from Herod. However Price summarises –

> 'I think we can conclude that between the money given Him by the wise men and the money He earned through work, Jesus of Nazareth

---

74 Price, *Prosperity: Good News for God's People*, p24
75 Ibid., p27

had a boatload of money when He entered His earthly ministry.'[76]

Christ needed this money according to Price because –

'for three and one-half years, Jesus knew He had to support twelve grown men – feed them, clothe them, pay their taxes, pay all transport fees ... pay all temple taxes and sacrifice fees and so on.'[77]

He is sure of this even though Luke tells us that it was the women who ministered to Jesus of their substance *(Luke 8.2-3)*. Price finds evidence that Jesus had money to spare in that he commanded his disciples to give to the poor and he would not fail to do so himself. He also draws the reasonable conclusion that the disciples were in the habit of giving to the poor, based on the assumption of the disciples that this is what Judas went to do *(John 13.29)*. Even if this is true, it does not imply that the Lord Jesus or his disciples had great wealth, for any such gifts are according to what we have and not according to what we do not have *(2 Corinthians 8.12)*. Price thinks he finds a clue to the scale of their giving in the remark about the worth of the alabaster flask of nard which could have been sold and the money given to the poor, but this is almost certainly an exceptional treasure in the household and not a sign of their habitual lifestyle. Price exaggerates to make a case, when he says –

'Somehow people get wrapped up in some pie-in-the-sky notions that Jesus just walked around and never ate, never slept, never paid any taxes, never had to buy sandals, or never had to do any of the things that ordinary men do.'[78]

Similarly he tells us that Peter, James, John and Andrew had fishing businesses, that Peter owned a house, that Matthew collected taxes for the Romans, and that he was able to hold a feast in his house for a great company of publicans and others *(Luke 5.29)*. He argues inconclusively from *John 7.53* that because 'every man went

---

76 Price, *Prosperity: Good News for God's People*, p28
77 Ibid., p28
78 Ibid., p31

unto his own house' the disciples presumably had houses of their own to go to. But this was near to Jerusalem, far from Galilee, and it is too much to believe that these Galileans all had a second home in the capital. The disciples had a treasurer, he says, and you don't need a treasurer unless you have treasure. All of this serves to show no more than that the disciples were properly organised and not living in poverty, but this is far from proving that they set us an example of pursuing wealth on earth.

Price finds evidence for the apostle Paul's wealth and Roman citizenship in his ability to pay the expenses of the four men being purified, and in the costs he would have incurred for his imprisonment and expensive lawsuits. He claims that a poor man would never have been given personal interviews with the likes of Felix, Princess Drusilla, and Queen Bernice. These remarks ignore the fact that Paul was sent to Felix at Caesarea, having been the victim of a plot against his life, that the Jews formally charged him, that Roman justice afforded him certain rights as a Roman citizen, that fame attracts attention, and that King Agrippa asked if he could see Paul rather than the other way around. If Felix hoped for a bribe to release Paul, we can assume that, 'knowing how the Christians aided one another in distress,'[79] he thought it would come from Paul's friends, not from Paul himself.

Leroy Thompson notes Paul's words, 'For ye know the grace of our Lord Jesus Christ, that, though he was rich, yet for your sakes he became poor, that ye through his poverty might be rich' *(2 Corinthians 8.9)*, and gives us his own theory of what this means. He informs us –

> 'Jesus became poor when He died on the cross as our Saviour, Redeemer and Substitute. That's when Jesus became poor – when He became a curse for us – not in His earthly ministry.'[80]

79 W. J. Conybeare and J. S. Howson, *The Life and Epistles of St Paul,* p611, Longmans, 1888
80 Thompson, *Money Cometh!* p246

To convince us of this he refers to various miracles of the Lord –

'In Jesus' earthly ministry, He ruled the laws of nature. I mean, Jesus could have guests of more than 5,000 and take five loaves and two fishes and feed them all! That doesn't sound very poor to me! And when it came to tax time, this "poor" Jesus told Peter, "You go catch a fish, and the first fish which you catch, reach in its mouth, and our tax money will be there." That doesn't sound poor to me!'[81]

The absurd and even outrageous suggestion being made here is that the Lord Jesus Christ used his miraculous powers to enrich himself materially. Hasn't this writer ever read how Satan tempted Christ to relieve his hunger by turning stones into bread? Christ dismissed this devious temptation by reminding Satan that obedience to God's Word is more important than the satisfying of bodily appetites. If the Lord rejected the suggestion that he use his powers to relieve his genuine bodily hunger, how much less would he use them to enrich himself financially!

Christ became poor not by contrast with human riches, but by contrast with the infinite riches which he possessed in Heaven before the incarnation. He was willing to become poor by appearing in the form of a man born in a low condition, with his divine glory hidden. Nevertheless the New Testament unquestionably teaches that he lived a simple lifestyle without any of the trappings of wealth; he did this in order to eliminate the possibility that any should follow him out of earthly ambition. The idea that he only experienced poverty on the cross is another unsupportable private theory. It sees the Lord Jesus as enjoying prosperity up to the time of his crucifixion, as if the few paltry possessions he had during his earthly life were worthy to be compared with the glories of Heaven that he had given up for our sakes.

At this point Thompson introduces us to a dangerous perversion of the atonement. He says –

'In Jesus' death on the cross, a great exchange took place. When Jesus

---

81 Thompson, *Money Cometh!* p246

became poor on the cross, in His great act of redemption, there was a place-swapping!'[82] 'Jesus took our place in poverty, but He didn't stay there any longer than three days! Having taken on the sinful state of man, he couldn't stand being broke any longer! He came up on the third day! He said, in effect, "Enough of this!" And He arose, victorious over death, hell and the grave, and over your poverty. Poverty should not keep you down any more since Jesus arose victorious over the devil and poverty!'[83]

What is so distasteful about these words is that they belittle the sufferings of Christ by having him shed his blood for something so worthless: to give Christians the passing things of this world rather than the eternal riches of Heaven. It is sickening to see such things put side by side. If Christ suffered poverty only in terms of earthly riches – so that we 'through his poverty might be rich' – why was something so precious used to purchase something so trivial? Peter says, 'Forasmuch as ye know that ye were not redeemed with corruptible things, as silver and gold, from your vain conversation received by tradition from your fathers; but with the precious blood of Christ, as of a lamb without blemish and without spot' *(1 Peter 1.18-19).* As gold could not purchase something as glorious as our redemption, neither did the precious blood of Christ purchase something so worthless as gold.

So what does the New Testament teach about the lifestyle of Christ and the apostles while on earth? Nowhere does it say that they were subject to constant poverty. What is recorded by all New Testament writers is that the Lord taught his disciples to live a simple lifestyle in dependence on God. The question of their financial background or even of their current earthly resources is beside the point, for they were men called to another lifestyle in imitation of their Lord.

Prosperity teachers are tired of having *Luke 9.58* quoted at them, and protest that it is used to suggest something that it not true of the Lord's life. Frederick Price trivially remarks that Jesus had a pillow

---

82 Ibid., p248
83 Ibid., p250

to rest his head on when asleep in the boat during the storm.[84] However when Jesus said, 'Foxes have holes, and birds of the air have nests; but the Son of man hath not where to lay his head,' his words cannot be made to mean the opposite of what he intended by crass literalism. This figure of speech means that during his public ministry on earth the Lord had nowhere that he could call home, for he was ever moving towards that final hour which would result in his return to Heaven above, which alone could ever be a sufficient resting place for him.

Some of the disciples who lived around Galilee had fishing businesses. Price wants us to see from the miraculous catch of fish that –

'in a few minutes, with Jesus, they caught more fish than they had in the last twenty-four hours. Jesus gave *[Peter]* a prosperity harvest: good measure, shaken together, and literally running over.'[85]

Always, the sublime is reduced to the ridiculous by these teachers. This was of course not a miracle intended to enhance Peter's fishing business, but to be a sign of the work which Christ was calling them to do as fishers of men. Besides, Luke tells us that 'when they had brought their ships to land, they forsook all, and followed him' *(Luke 5.11)*, and turned their backs on their former business concerns. This was not simply the act of a moment, easily reversed, but was the start of a new life of discipleship, for Peter sometime later asks the Lord, 'Behold, we have forsaken all, and followed thee; what shall we have therefore?' *(Matthew 19.27)*. Why make reference to irrelevant facts in trying to build a case for prosperity?

Christ sent out his disciples with clear instructions, 'Provide neither gold, nor silver, nor brass in your purses, nor scrip for your journey, neither two coats, neither shoes, nor yet staves' *(Matthew 10.9-10)*. Certainly it was not their normal practice to be without

---

84 Price, *Prosperity: Good News for God's People*, p24
85 Ibid., p79

money and therefore this instruction marked a change from their normal habit, but this does not justify Price's conclusion that 'this was a test, not of the disciples, but of those who would hear *[their]* message,'[86] for the disciples were being taught to live by faith and to depend on God's providential supply of all their needs. They needed to learn that 'the labourer is worthy of his hire' *(Luke 10.7)*. This is very clear from the Lord's subsequent question and their answer: 'And he said unto them, When I sent you without purse, and scrip, and shoes, lacked ye any thing? And they said, Nothing' *(Luke 22.35)*.

This instruction sets a pattern for all missions throughout the church age, for the messenger of God must be above suspicion, and must not be open to the charge of serving the Gospel for 'filthy lucre' *(1 Timothy 3.3, 8)*. This was why Paul was anxious that the Thessalonians recognise that he did not come to them using 'a cloak of covetousness' *(1 Thessalonians 2.5)*; anything other than a simple lifestyle would risk doing this. For this reason Paul took very careful precautions to prevent misunderstanding when he went to Corinth. Although he insisted on his right to receive material support from them, he was unwilling to avail himself of this right: 'Nevertheless we have not used this power; but suffer all things, lest we should hinder the gospel of Christ' *(1 Corinthians 9.11-12, 14)*. As an apostle he was entitled to live by the Gospel, but he had deliberately avoided asking this of young believers or those seeking the Lord in Corinth, lest they draw the wrong conclusion and the Gospel be maligned.

11 – Tithing as a means of getting rich

It is not uncommon for those in Prosperity Gospel churches to receive a weekly lecture on the subject of tithing, and to be exhorted on this subject in a completely disproportionate manner, given that this is only a part of the spectrum of teaching to be honoured by the Christian church.

---

86 Ibid., p31

Many prosperity teachers look back to Oral Roberts as the one who most firmly established the link between tithing and prosperity. Roberts tells us —

> 'It came to me with an impact I felt through my entire being: Jesus as the seed God planted ... Gradually the picture became clearer. My Blessing-Pact Partnership was based on my faith in Him. To meet my needs I could regularly, either weekly or monthly, make my Seed-Faith giving an act of my believing; I could release it toward God ... The idea of SEED-FAITH was born in my heart that day when I saw that everything God does starts with a seed planted.'[87]

Roberts reminds us that he discovered three key principles at work in the Blessing-Pact Partnership: 1. God is your source; 2. Give that it may be given unto you; and 3. Expect a miracle.

The first principle sounds safe enough until we ask, 'What is God the source of?' The Christian is of course dependent on the Lord for everything, but Roberts' message to the church is that God is also the source of material wealth for his people, which begs the question of whether God is willing to give wealth to all his people. He says —

> 'If you want God to supply your financial needs, then give SEED-MONEY for Him to reproduce and multiply.'[88] 'Only what you give can God multiply back to you again.'[89]

The second principle (give that it may be given unto you) supplies us with a seriously flawed motive for giving. Even the greatest acts of self-sacrifice, Paul tells us, are worth nothing if done for the wrong motive. 'Though I bestow all my goods to feed the poor ... and have not charity, it profiteth me nothing' (1 Corinthians 13.3). The motive presented to us by Roberts is entirely selfish. We should give in order that we may receive, and what we expect to receive is more of what we gave. Matthew Ashimolowo in a discussion on giving states —

> 'God has put in place an inviolable law that seed must produce after

---

87 Oral Roberts, *Miracles of Seed-Faith*, pp12-13, Oral Roberts Evangelistic Association, 1982

88 Ibid., p25

89 Ibid., p24

its own kind ... Giving is the planting of the financial seed in order to experience a financial harvest ... The greatest consequence of not giving to God is financial barrenness.'[90]

In the light of the deceitfulness of the human heart, this teaching is fatal to any form of unselfish or sacrificial giving to God. Believers should, in obedience and love to God, let go of any expectation of receiving from God in kind. The cure of covetousness is indeed to give, but the reward such givers should look for is benefit to others and blessing in Heaven. The sort of return that prosperity teachers encourage us to expect is closer to the return that comes from an investment in the financial world, than to the reward that God gives. God's reward always teaches us to look to Heaven and away from the passing things of this world.

In *John 6*, we read of those who saw the miracle of the feeding of the five thousand and were so impressed that they searched diligently for Christ, wanting to make him king by force. On finding him back in Capernaum, they showed great interest in how he managed to cross Galilee unnoticed. The Lord however dismissed their interest in finding him as insignificant. He could see into their hearts and knew they were fleshly. They could see no further than to make him an earthly king, to bring them prosperity, but he had come to establish the kingdom of Heaven. With devastating effect he exposed what lay in their hearts, saying, 'Verily, verily, I say unto you, Ye seek me, not because ye saw the miracles, but because ye did eat of the loaves, and were filled. Labour not for the meat which perisheth, but for that meat which endureth unto everlasting life, which the Son of man shall give unto you' *(John 6.26-27)*.

Their minds were set on earthly bread when he had come to give them heavenly bread. Their first desire destroyed the second, for it is impossible to find Christ as Saviour if motivated by desire for earthly gain. And yet, the Prosperity Gospel preaches earthly riches

---

90 Ashimolowo, *The Coming Wealth Transfer*, pp 192-193, 207

in the here and now. These teachers would protest that they also preach about eternal salvation, but if this message is there at all, it gets lost in the other. Christ warns us that it is so hard to detach men and women from their addiction to this world, that the Gospel has to be presented in the clearest of terms as a message of spiritual blessing, and any confusion on this matter is fatal to the truth. What harm the Prosperity Gospel has done in obscuring the Gospel by merging it with financial salvation!

The third principle Roberts teaches (expect a miracle) detracts from the meaning of the word miracle. A miracle is a rare but genuine suspension of the laws of nature which otherwise operate with constant regularity as God governs the world. The miracles Roberts has in mind here are the provision of material gain as a reward for service to God. Prayer is made an Aladdin's lamp to give us whatever we want.

Other writers have developed this idea. John Avanzini writes –

'Jesus tells us the kingdom of God has seed-power. "It is like a grain of mustard seed..." God has given seed-power to the money you give into the Gospel...Your money-seed has the potential of bringing forth a money harvest...When you give your hard-earned money into the Gospel, God looks at it as a money-seed, thereby giving the potential for massive multiplication.'[91]

This, however, is all self-seeking, whereas sincere giving, like sowing of seed, results in a spiritual harvest and a reward stored up for them in Heaven 'where neither moth nor rust doth corrupt, and where thieves do not break through nor steal' *(Matthew 6.20)*.

In a chapter entitled 'Wisdom: The Key Ingredient to Financial Success',[92] Creflo Dollar claims that God's reward of material wealth to Solomon was the result of his seeking wisdom. Dollar would have his readers seek wealth, despite Scripture telling us that Solomon was commended for not seeking it.

---

91 Avanzini, *What Jesus Taught About Manifesting Abundance*, pp 27, 30
92 Dollar, *The Holy Spirit, Your Financial Advisor*, p73

Money is a subject which preoccupies these writers. Matthew Ashimolowo has chapters covering 62 pages in his book, *The Coming Wealth Transfer* entitled, 'Investment', 'Portfolio Management', 'Wealth', 'Reinvestment', and 'Multi-Generational Wealth'. In case anyone makes the mistake of thinking that there is some spiritual application in all this, it is necessary to point out that apart from a few unrelated texts, these chapters are pure financial advice.

Prosperity teachers often present tithing as a safeguard against the love of money, but they forget that the Pharisees were noted for their tithing, yet this did not stop them being filled with covetousness. Christ said to them, 'Woe unto you, scribes and Pharisees, hypocrites! for ye pay tithe of mint and anise and cummin, and have omitted the weightier matters of the law, judgment, mercy, and faith,' and he immediately afterwards added, 'Woe unto you, scribes and Pharisees, hypocrites! for ye make clean the outside of the cup and of the platter, but within they are full of extortion and excess' *(Matthew 23.23-25)*. In their case, tithing and covetousness went hand in hand.

Tithing brings prosperity, or so Frederick Price tells us. He quotes *Proverbs 3.9-10*, 'Honour the Lord with thy substance, and with the firstfruits of all thine increase: so shall thy barns be filled with plenty, and thy presses shall burst out with new wine.' According to him the modern equivalent to this is –

> **'Give the Lord honour through your possessions by giving Him the first of your profits from your work or business, so that your bank accounts will be large and your stock portfolios will keep on growing.'**[93]

These writers constantly fail to translate the language of the old covenant into the terms of the new. Leroy Thompson discourages Christians from asking any questions about who they give to. He says –

---

93 Price, *Prosperity: Good News for God's People*, p71

'Some people ... say, "Well, I'm not giving my tithe, because I don't know what that church will do with my money." But, really, your business is to give your tithe and expect God to bless you. If something is wrong in that church, God will handle it.'[94]

While Christians should not be suspicious minded, it is right that they look carefully at what is being done with the funds they steward to the Lord. The leaders of any congregation have a duty to give an account to their members of how they have used the gifts of the Lord's people, and this is done partly to satisfy God's people that their gifts are being handled wisely and honestly, and spiritually. When so many have been exposed as charlatans, it is our responsibility to make sure that we give only to those who love and stand by the true Gospel and who administer our gifts with integrity.

12 – Perverting the Christian life

The life which prosperity teachers present as normal for the Christian is unrecognisable to the vast majority of Bible believers. We have seen how these writers set an expectation in the minds of God's people that they should not experience any hardship in financial matters. Kenneth Hagin recounts how in his early ministry he faced financial hardship –

'During that first year on the field, my clothes and my car had worn out. The car had four bald tyres and no spare ... With the little that was left, we bought some school clothes for the children. That left us with virtually nothing.'[95]

He learnt that this hardship was unnecessary. God told him –

'Faith is the same in the financial realm as it is in any of the others ... If it were healing you needed for your own body, you would claim it by faith ... You have to do the same thing when it comes to finances.'[96]

Matthew Ashimolowo is concerned about the problem of debt

---

94 Thompson, *Money Cometh!* p137
95 Hagin, *How God Taught Me About Prosperity*, p6
96 Ibid., pp10-11

in the churches – for instance in holding a 25-year mortgage – and again teaches that God's people need not live like this.

> 'We know He is a debt cancelling God. When the prophets went out to cut wood, an axe head fell into the river – that instrument of commerce with which wood was chopped to feed a family. God caused the axe head to swim again. When the widow who was left broke, busted and disgusted by her husband who probably held views against the personal prosperity of God's people, it required a debt cancelling God to bring her and her children out of it. "She went and told the man of God, and he said, 'Go, sell the oil and pay your debts. You and your sons can live on what is left.'" (2 Kings 4.7)' [97]

Scripture presents these two events as singular miracles with lessons about God's ability to retrieve what is irretrievably lost in the spiritual realm, and to provide for the spiritual needs of his people, but Ashimolowo uses them to teach all Christians to expect the same relief from their material debts today.

The Bible's portrayal of the Christian life is very different, both in its trials and hardships, and its consolations. Many verses speak of the cost of discipleship and that cost is often experienced in terms of loss of earthly comforts. At Paul's conversion, Ananias was told by the Lord concerning the apostle's future ministry, 'I will shew him how great things he must suffer for my name's sake' (Acts 9.16). His life was full of triumphs in the Gospel as God used him to establish churches across Asia Minor and beyond, but there was a price to pay for his instrumentality, and in some of the more personal passages in his letters he shares with the churches what that cost had been: 'For we would not, brethren, have you ignorant of our trouble which came to us in Asia, that we were pressed out of measure, above strength, insomuch that we despaired even of life: but we had the sentence of death in ourselves, that we should not trust in ourselves, but in God which raiseth the dead' (2 Corinthians 1.8-9). This was not an isolated experience but was repeated throughout his life.

In summing up his calling, Paul says, 'But in all things approving

---

97 Ashimolowo, *The Coming Wealth Transfer*, p35

ourselves as the ministers of God, in much patience, in afflictions, in necessities, in distresses, in stripes, in imprisonments, in tumults, in labours, in watchings, in fastings . . .' *(2 Corinthians 6.4-5)*.

His work for the Lord meant that he must often not only suffer beatings, prison, and fearful riots, but hardship in the form of the need to work to support himself, and shortage of sleep and food; this was not voluntary fasting connected with prayer, but lack of provision which resulted in hunger.

He commends the Philippians because they recognised his lack and 'sent once and again unto my necessity' *(Philippians 4.16)*. Were these the privations of a man who failed to understand the Prosperity Gospel and neglected to claim the promises of earthly wealth to which he was entitled? After all, according to the strange views of prosperity teachers, Paul was also in the new covenant which is supposed to bring Christians the material blessings given to Abraham.

In the same passage Paul describes himself as 'poor, yet making many rich; as having nothing, and yet possessing all things' *(2 Corinthians 6.10)*. Evidently he did not have or need material riches as he went about doing the Lord's work, and relied upon the support of others, and yet he made many rich. With what did he make them rich? Not with this world's wealth for he had none to give, nor did he make them rich by preaching a Gospel of earthly prosperity to them, for if that was his message he was a signal failure by his own example.

Later in the same epistle Paul tells us that as he journeyed with the precious Gospel, crossing land and seas to reach needy souls, he was often, 'in perils of waters, in perils of robbers, in perils by mine own countrymen, in perils by the heathen, in perils in the city, in perils in the wilderness, in perils in the sea, in perils among false brethren; in weariness and painfulness, in watchings often, in hunger and thirst, in fastings often, in cold and nakedness' *(2 Corinthians 11.26-27)*.

How foolish to think that he did not understand the message

which Hagin, Copeland, Jakes and others teach, that Christians were never expected to know hardship of this sort. According to them, even if Paul had to endure beatings for Christ, he certainly did not need to go hungry or thirsty, without adequate clothing, or without money in his purse!

Were these sufferings only experienced by apostles and others called to the ministry, but not by rank-and-file Christians? By no means, for the New Testament warns all believers what to expect in this world and offers comfort to all. The Lord Jesus described the nature of the Christian life when he prepared his people for the life of discipleship: 'Blessed are ye, when men shall revile you, and persecute you, and shall say all manner of evil against you falsely, for my sake. Rejoice, and be exceeding glad: for great is your reward in heaven: for so persecuted they the prophets which were before you' *(Matthew 5.11-12)*.

We read how the Old Testament prophets were treated by their unbelieving countrymen, and we note that they suffered not only rejection and violence, but also deprivation for the sake of the Word of God. This is what Christ prepares his disciples to expect. Bible prophecy teaches that God's people can expect to be disadvantaged in this life and, far from controlling the wealth of this world, to be like the prophets before them, who 'wandered about in sheepskins and goatskins; being destitute, afflicted, tormented; (of whom the world was not worthy:) they wandered in deserts, and in mountains, and in dens and caves of the earth' *(Hebrews 11.37-38)*. Do modern followers of the prosperity movement aspire to be greater than the cloud of witnesses that went before them?

Paul pictures believers as being willing to forfeit many things that the world enjoys in order to remain faithful to Christ, including material comforts and security: 'If in this life only we have hope in Christ, we are of all men most miserable' *(1 Corinthians 15.19)*. This is not just about a theoretical belief in the resurrection, but about the life that such a belief makes one willing to live. In his own case he could say, 'I die daily. If after the manner of men I have fought with beasts at Ephesus, what advantageth it me, if the dead rise not?' *(1 Corinthians 15.31-32)*. But why would Christians be of all men the most miserable? Because in coming to Christ, they are ready to give up the riches and advantages of this life if necessary and to lose what the world enjoys, and if there is no compensation in the world to come, all this is for nothing. The Christians addressed in *Hebrews 10.34* were reminded – 'Ye ... took joyfully the spoiling of your goods, knowing in yourselves that ye have in heaven a better and an enduring substance.'

What were the things that mattered to Paul, and what upheld him in all his trials? Not the thought of earthly riches which prosperity teachers treat as so essential, but the work that God had given him to do. For Paul, all that he endured was worthwhile because of the fruit that came in the form of men, women, and children gathered into the kingdom of Heaven and saved for all eternity. It was the Philippians' success in 'holding forth the word of life' that would cause him to 'rejoice in the day of Christ, that I have not run in vain, neither laboured in vain' *(Philippians 2.16)*, and he calls them 'my joy and crown' *(Philippians 4.1)*. Similarly he says to the Thessalonians, 'For what is our hope, or joy, or crown of rejoicing? Are not even ye in the presence of our Lord Jesus Christ at his coming? For ye are our glory and joy' *(1 Thessalonians 2.19-20)*.

Church history bears out this picture. It shows us millions of God's people who have been willing to suffer the loss of all things in this life and experience disadvantages in order that they hold on to Christ. He does not protect them from all loss, because men must know that they count him worth more than anything this world has to offer. By stark contrast Joel Osteen tells us –

'Stop limiting God. He may want to open another opportunity or a better position for you. God may intervene in your situation, replacing your supervisor so you can be promoted. One day, you may run that entire company! Once you begin expecting more, a second key element to enlarging your vision is believing that God has more in store for you!'[98]

13 – Making wealth the mark of God's approval

Prosperity teachers strongly imply that it is possible to read God's favour or displeasure towards his people in the degree of wealth which he has either given to them or witheld from them. Just as they transport the blessings of the old covenant directly into the new, so they transport its curses. Kenneth Copeland quotes the threatenings of the law made against Israel in *Deuteronomy 28.31* and comments, 'To lose everything – your job, your assets and your possessions – without any way to get them back, is a curse.'[99] When he uses the word 'curse', he does not simply mean that this is a painful experience, but that God has shown his displeasure towards us. But was God displeased with Job when he allowed Satan to take his possessions, his family, his health from him? It was the comforters who were incapable of judging the situation rightly and who concluded that Job must be a hypocrite, measured by his outward circumstances. They had to learn that material prosperity is no reliable marker of God's favour.

The psalmist was troubled when he saw how God allowed the wicked to prosper, when they showed disregard for his name. In comparing his lot with theirs, he began to draw wrong conclusions about God's love towards him, and about the wisdom of living a godly life. It was not until he realised that the prosperity of the wicked was theirs only for a moment, and that the true measure of God's love is his eternal favour, that he understood. It may often be the case that in this life the wicked seem to prosper more than the righteous, but the coming of the Lord will make all clear: 'As a dream when one awaketh; so, O Lord, when thou awakest, thou shalt despise their image' *(Psalm 73.20)*.

---

98 Joel Osteen, *Your Best Life Now*, p28, Hodder & Stoughton, 2008
99 Copeland, *Prosperity: The Choice is Yours*, p32

It was Solomon's conclusion that in this life no one can distinguish the righteous from the wicked by their outward circumstances, for he says, 'There is a vanity which is done upon the earth; that there be just men, unto whom it happeneth according to the work of the wicked; again, there be wicked men, to whom it happeneth according to the work of the righteous: I said that this also is vanity' *(Ecclesiastes 8.14).*

So why do prosperity teachers tell us that believers ought to be seen to be the ones to enjoy the good things of this world, and God is in the process of transferring wealth from the wicked to the righteous? Have they never read the Bible's explanation? Not material circumstances but godliness of heart indicates the true child of God.

Nothing that Paul suffered could convince him that God's love for him had diminished in the slightest degree, and he teaches all believers to make the same evaluation: 'Who shall separate us from the love of Christ? shall tribulation, or distress, or persecution, or famine, or nakedness, or peril, or sword?...I am persuaded, that neither death, nor life, nor angels, nor principalities, nor powers, nor things present, nor things to come, nor height, nor depth, nor any other creature, shall be able to separate us from the love of God, which is in Christ Jesus our Lord' *(Romans 8.35-39).*

14 – Ridiculing Christian contentment

In his letter to the church at Philippi, the apostle Paul tells them that it is a source of great joy to him that their material support for him has flourished again, so that they have provided for his bodily needs and helped advance the cause of Christ through his preaching. What causes him such gladness is not that he has personally benefited from their gift, but that they have recognised the surpassing importance of the Gospel and have been ready to give to the Lord at personal cost to themselves. This, Paul knows, is a good work that is pleasing to God and will abound to their eternal account. At the same time, he is at pains to explain that even though he suffered shortage for a while, he was not anxious or complaining towards God, nor did he despair as to how God would provide for him.

Even in his great need he was trusting the Lord and confident that God would supply his need. He assures them, 'Not that I speak in respect of want: for I have learned, in whatsoever state I am, therewith to be content. I know both how to be abased, and I know how to abound: every where and in all things I am instructed both to be full and to be hungry, both to abound and to suffer need. I can do all things through Christ which strengtheneth me' *(Philippians 4.11-13)*. The secret of contentment is something that God had taught him and the reason he was so keen to share this with them was that they too should understand this secret, for contentment in all circumstances should be the aim of all believers.

One of the many problems with the Prosperity Gospel is that it makes this sort of contentment impossible, for while the apostle taught that contentment is a comfort and a safeguard in all situations, prosperity teachers tell us that poverty is a curse, that there can be little joy in a state of need, and that God wills that no Christian should remain in it. Thompson says –

> 'Being broke is a curse; it's not a blessing. You don't have to have the mind of a genius to figure that out. When you're broke, your car is out of gas, your refrigerator is empty, your baby is crying because he's hungry and your spouse is grouchy because of debt, distress and discontentment – that is a curse! It's terrible to be broke!'[100]

There is no evidence here that he has even started to learn Paul's secret.

Frederick Price offers us contentment, but on a completely wrong basis. He says –

> 'Now you can take your financial appeals directly to God. *Philippians 4.6* tells us, "Be anxious for nothing, but in everything by prayer and supplication, with thanksgiving, let your requests be made known to God." OK, then what, Paul? "And my God shall supply all your need

---

100 Thompson, *Money Cometh!* p251

according to His riches in glory by Christ Jesus" *(Philippians 4.19).*
Thanks to the new covenant, not only do we have a right to the blessings of Abraham, all of the blessings of the psalmist, but now anything
that wasn't directly covered in those promises we can take to God
directly ... There is not one thing that you can need that God will not
supply you.'[101]

Paul tells us in verses 11-12 of this chapter that he has been taught
the secret of contentment in every situation, whether he has much
or little, whether he is full or hungry. He is content in the midst of
want just as much as in the midst of plenty. But what Price is saying
is quite different. He also tells us that we can be content, but for
him contentment comes only because God supplies our need and
gives us whatever we ask for. This is why he brings the Abrahamic
covenant into his argument and the idea that all the material promises made to Abraham belong to the new covenant also. For him,
freedom from anxiety comes because we are denied nothing. That is
not contentment in the midst of need. For Paul, contentment comes
because he has surrendered all his anxieties into the hands of his
heavenly Father who he knows by faith will not fail to provide what
is right for him.

The version of contentment taught by Price is the only version that
many in the Word of Faith movement understand, for it is evident
from their writings that they find a state of scarcity deeply upset-
ting. Many of them have come from poor backgrounds and speak of
their past deprivation with strong emotion. They have 'discovered'
the prosperity teaching as a release from this former hardship and
wish to hold onto it and defend it for all they are worth. They have
concocted a theology to justify it, but it is obvious they never learned
Paul's contentment in their former situation, and they never wish to
return to that state again. Tragically this leads to an abandonment of
moderation, as is evident from remarks by Thompson –

'If you are broke and in debt, are you ready to come out of that

---

101 Price, *Prosperity: Good News for God's People*, p104

condition? Are you ready to quit standing in line at stores with your credit card, wondering if it is going to "go through" and be approved? That's not for the Body of Christ! That's poverty. But I'm sharing some things with you that you can put into practice, and eventually you'll get to the place where you can go into a store and buy anything you want. When you go somewhere to try on suits, for example, you're just going to say what size you want, go into the dressing room, put it on, come back out and lead the salesperson to the cash register – all without asking how much the suit costs – because you are part of the Body of Christ!' [102]

Soon the main source of happiness becomes material things –

'If you want what God wants you to have, then pay careful attention to what I'm about to show you in *Psalm 35.27*, "Let them shout for joy, and be glad, that favour my righteous cause: yea, let them say continually, let the Lord be magnified, which hath pleasure in the prosperity of his servant."...I tell you, when you're in God's divine program financially, it brings joy and gladness!' [103]

15 – Stimulating the love of money

In an extended passage in *1 Timothy 6*, Paul instructs Timothy and all Christians what our attitude to material riches should be. In contrast to those who suppose 'that gain is godliness' (verse 5), Timothy is to understand that 'godliness with contentment is great gain' (verse 6). The word 'contentment' means literally 'self-sufficiency', but in a good sense, not needing anything from the world because we are content with what God has given us and we trust him to supply all our need, whether we have much or little. Such an attitude makes us independent of our circumstances, because God is the source of all we need and he will not fail us. It also makes us willing to leave to God's wisdom the matter of how much we receive in this world. God who knows our weakness will not give us material blessings which we are not able to handle. If he chooses to give us little in this life, then we are confident that

---

102 Thompson, *Money Cometh!* p36
103 Ibid., p15

this will work for the best. While some see godliness as a means of material gain (because they see everything as a means of material gain, since their minds are focused on this world), Scripture teaches that godliness is true spiritual gain when it is combined with material contentment. The Christian can afford to be content because he possesses far more unseen riches than the worldling is capable of imagining. This more than makes up for any shortage in this life.

With Job's words in mind Paul reminds us that, 'we brought nothing into this world, and it is certain we can carry nothing out' (verse 7). We have started from nothing, and all that we gain during life must again be reduced to nothing at the end of life, for we cannot take with us any of the things we have gained during life. Even before we leave this world we begin to lose the ability to enjoy such things as we have. As far as we are concerned, earthly riches are passing away, just as they are passing away in themselves, because heaven and earth will pass away. For anyone to make their possessions the chief source of their pleasure is bound to bring a terrible sense of loss at the point of death. Why then is earthly prosperity something that should be regarded as essential or a God-given right for believers?

'And having food and raiment let us be therewith content' (verse 8). Here is the level on which we should set our sights. The care of the body with the essentials of life is what we are entitled to pray for, and even for these things Christ has taught us to trust God, and not to be anxious when we cannot see the means by which they will be supplied. Our lives are in the hands of God, and he knows what is necessary to support life.

By complete contrast the Prosperity Gospel urges us not to be content with bread and raiment but to ask God for more. T. D. Jakes is well aware of this passage in *1 Timothy* and seems to accept what Paul teaches –

'**Profit comes when the faithful are contented, not being led by the lust of success nor driven by the promise of wealth, but calmly** assured that God knows the whens, the whos, and the hows of blessing his people. Verse 7 assures us that nothing tangible is eternal. No matter what we have attained, none of it is transportable to where we are going.'[104]

But all too soon he begins to struggle against this position. Like all prosperity teachers, he wants to be seen to do justice to the Word of God. He cannot ignore passages like this, which speak so powerfully against his position, so he has to make a show of respect for them. But he really wants to teach a doctrine which is completely at odds with this, and ends up with a thoroughly inconsistent message, saying:

> 'I want to prove that God is not against us being affluent. Through our sacrifice and giving, He honours with a hundredfold return. This return is not in Heaven; as Jesus plainly promised, a hundredfold return will be gained in this life! Why would I need a hundredfold return in Heaven? I need the return on my investment in this life while still recognising that the greater wealth is still, as he so aptly puts it, eternal life.'[105]

But God's Word draws the line at the desire to be rich: 'But they that will be rich fall into temptation and a snare, and into many foolish and hurtful lusts, which drown men in destruction and perdition' (verse 9). What is forbidden here is not the possession of riches (those who are already rich are addressed in verse 17), but the aspiration to be rich. This is something that prosperity teachers are constantly trying to skirt around because it cuts right across their teaching. Leroy Thompson attempts to qualify these words –

> 'A person could be as godly and contented without money as he could be with it. But he could be more contented with some money in his pocket!...'But they that will be rich...' (1 Timothy 6.9). That means they want to be rich for the wrong purpose and with the wrong attitude about money.' [106]

---

104 Jakes, *The Great Investment*, p27
105 Ibid., p28
106 Thompson, *Money Cometh!* pp178, 180

It is OK for the individual to want to be rich, according to Thompson, but he must have the right attitude towards riches. However, we play games with God's Word at our peril, for it is too easy to deceive ourselves about our motive for wanting something. The desire to be rich, Paul warns, is something that rapidly gets out of control, and causes much hurt or damage to the one who plays with it. At no point in his quest for riches does the acquisitive man have contentment, so he can never reach an end of desiring more. Solomon warned of this sinister disease of the soul: 'There is one alone, and there is not a second; yea, he hath neither child nor brother: yet is there no end of all his labour; neither is his eye satisfied with riches; neither saith he, For whom do I labour, and bereave my soul of good?' *(Ecclesiastes 4.8)*. To desire riches for the sake of the Lord's work while at the same time wanting the benefits of wealth for our personal gratification is an impossible balancing act. We cannot serve God and mammon.

'For the love of money is the root of all evil: which while some coveted after, they have erred from the faith, and pierced themselves through with many sorrows' (verse 10). Truly this verse tells us that not money, but the love of money, is a root of all kinds of evil and prosperity teachers never tire of pointing this out. But having ignored Scripture's boundary line and justified the desire to be rich, it is impossible that the love of money does not enter their hearts. Is there not love of money when Benny Hinn can promise –

> 'Imagine not dreading going to the mailbox, no bills piling up on your counter, and no calls from collectors coming to your home. God wants to wipe your debt out! Every bit of it . . . and in the next 90 days!'[107]

Is there not a love of money when Joel Osteen encourages ever bigger material requests to God –

> 'We say, "God, would you please give me a slightly bigger flat? I don't want to bother you for too much." No, God wants to give you your

---

107 http://www.bennyhinn.org/emailletters/9236/breaking-the-bondage-of-debt-during-the-next-90-days

own house...He's not having financial difficulties. He owns it all. Why not believe Him for bigger things?'[108]

Or when John Avanzini tells us that the church has reached a time of financial abundance –

'It is over and above time in the financial realm. The church has reached the time of superabundance. Those who will enter are those who are willing to believe the Word of God concerning biblical prosperity.'[109]

Money has an unrivalled power to remove misery according to Frederick Price –

'Many people have dreams of what they would like to achieve in life, and I can say with virtual certainty that everything they dream of costs money...It's also true that most of those things that make us unhappy stem from a shortage of money.'[110]

We should not try to impose a uniform standard on all people in the church. Ministers cannot tell their congregations that no one should ever move to a bigger house or get a bigger car, for our needs change, and things deteriorate and need replacing. But we should never upgrade for the sake of looking special, or for status, so that we are thought to be successful by others. Neither should we try to surround ourselves with all that we need on earth, or create for ourselves an earthly utopia like the landowner in Christ's parable, who on receiving a bumper harvest pulled down his barns and built bigger ones *(Luke 12.18)*. Nor should we gather possessions for the mere pleasure of possessing them, for this is to make an idol of created things.

Fallen human nature has a tendency to transfer trust from God to material things the moment our earthly goods increase. Therefore Paul warns, 'Charge them that are rich in this world, that they be not highminded, nor trust in uncertain riches, but in the living God,

---

108 Osteen, *Your Best Life Now*, pp45-46
109 Avanzini, *What Jesus Taught About Manifesting Abundance*, p7
110 Price, *Prosperity: Good News for God's People*, p40

who giveth us richly all things to enjoy' *(1 Timothy 6.17)*. For this reason, those who have wealth have to take particular care in watching their hearts. Certainly, it will be a protection to them to treat what they have as belonging to the Lord and at his disposal, so that they are ready to give to those in need without any reluctance. Paul does not tell the rich to give away all their riches, but he does tell them not to be high-minded, nor to allow a sense of superiority to develop in them.

16 – A heresy to be avoided

The Prosperity Gospel presents us with a radically different version of Christianity from that taught in the Bible. Although some (not all) teachers in this movement try to hold on to the essence of the Gospel, their false emphasis on wealth has an immensely distorting effect on their lifestyle and the lifestyle of those within their churches, and this is bound to injure the message they preach. In some prosperity churches there are evidently true believers who are struggling with this teaching, and are deeply uncomfortable with it, but who do not know where to turn. But others have sold out to a message which promises them Heaven without having to part company with the world and its pleasures.

We have seen that this teaching is justified by a desperate misreading of God's promises to Abraham. Prosperity teachers take the earthly, material promises given to Abraham's descendants and treat these as if they were of permanent character, rather than temporary symbols of far more precious and eternal spiritual riches. Failing to view the Bible primarily as a spiritual book, they reduce its message to the level of the physical, and misunderstand God's teaching method by which the earthly benefits of old stand for something far more abiding. In this way they lead God's people into covetousness and ensnare many in the love of money. While, as shepherds of Christ's flock, they ought to faithfully warn against the spiritual dangers associated with seeking gain in this life, they become instruments of the devil in ensnaring the unwary, and at the same time shamefully enrich themselves. By sleight of hand, they link tithing to personal enrichment in a way that allows them to cream off vast sums for themselves.

But who is deceiving who? At first sight, it seems to be the prosperity teacher who should be blamed for his distortion of the Gospel, but then deceiver and deceived appear to encourage each other. As the people are misled by teachers who urge them into covetousness, so the teachers become trapped by the approval and appreciation of a thoroughly carnal people. Both are comfortable with the arrangement that allows the prosperity preacher to say, 'Give some of your riches to the church and salve your conscience so that you may indulge yourself with the rest.'

For those who are troubled by this movement, whose souls long to be fed by the pure milk of the Word, and who recognise that they have been starved spiritually under prosperity teaching, may they find courage to separate from its false and destructive doctrine, and seek churches where the spiritual message of the Bible is honoured and proclaimed. In this way they can become the strong believers they ought to be, and begin to bear genuine fruit to the glory of God, bringing blessing on themselves and all around them.

May our outlook be that of John Newton's hymn –

> *Saviour, if of Zion's city,*
> *I through grace a member am,*
> *Let the world deride or pity,*
> *I will glory in Thy name:*
> *Fading is the worldling's pleasure,*
> *All his boasted pomp and show!*
> *Solid joys and lasting treasure,*
> *None but Zion's children know.*

'If ye then be risen with Christ, seek those
things which are above, where Christ sitteth on the right hand
of God. Set your affection on things above, not on things
on the earth' (Colossians 3.1-2).

ALSO BY ROBIN COMPSTON

Richard Dawkins' Fictional World

32 pages, booklet, Sword & Trowel, ISBN 978 1 899046 38 6

Richard Dawkins' book *The God Delusion* has sold in millions, attacking the God of the Bible with a ferocity not seen since the heyday of aggressive communism. But these assaults contain numerous mistakes, as many noted reviewers have pointed out.

'In this brief and readable response, the author exposes with exceptional clarity major mistakes, and at the same time shows the reality and value of the faith under attack.'

The Personal Spiritual Life
127 pages, paperback, ISBN 978 1 908919 20 5

From the personal indwelling of the Holy Spirit to living a life of commitment these chapters stir and encourage readers to advance spiritually.

In what sense may we 'feel' the presence of the Lord? What was the apostle Paul's method for progress in holiness? How may we identify our spiritual gifts? And how may we count more for the Lord, and sustain spiritual joy?

These are among the themes of this tonic for present-day disciples of Christ.

The Lord's Pattern for Prayer
118 pages, paperback, ISBN 978 1 870855 36 5

Subtitled – 'Studying the lessons and spiritual encouragements in the most famous of all prayers.' This volume is almost a manual on prayer, providing a real spur to the devotional life. The Lord's own plan and agenda for prayer – carefully amplified – takes us into the presence of the Father, to prove the privileges and power of God's promises to those who pray.

Chapters cover each petition in the Lord's Prayer. Here, too, are sections on remedies for problems in prayer, how to intercede for others, the reasons why God keeps us waiting for answers, and the nature of the prayer of faith.

God's Rules for Holiness
Unlocking the Ten Commandments
139 pages, paperback, ISBN 978 1 870855 37 2

Taken at face value the Ten Commandments are binding on all people, and will guard the way to Heaven, so that evil will never spoil its glory and purity. But the Commandments are far greater than their surface meaning, as this book shows.

They challenge us as Christians on a still wider range of sinful deeds and attitudes. They provide positive virtues as goals. And they give immense help for staying close to the Lord in our walk and worship.

The Commandments are vital for godly living and for greater blessing, but we need to enter into the panoramic view they provide for the standards and goals for redeemed people.

Faith, Doubts, Trials and Assurance
139 pages, paperback, ISBN 978 1 870855 50 1

Ongoing faith is essential for answered prayer, effective service, spiritual stability and real communion with God. In this book many questions are answered about faith, such as – How may we assess the state of our faith? How can faith be strengthened? What are the most dangerous doubts? How should difficult doubts be handled? What is the biblical attitude to trials? How can we tell if troubles are intended to chastise or to refine? What can be done to obtain assurance? What are the sources of assurance? Can a believer commit the unpardonable sin? Exactly how is the Lord's presence felt?

Dr Masters provides answers, with much pastoral advice, drawing on Scripture throughout.

Steps for Guidance
In the Journey of Life
134 pages, paperback, ISBN 978 1 870855 66 2

In recent years the subject of how to find God's guidance has become controversial. Some say that God does not have a specific plan for the lives of his people, but allows us to please ourselves. Others say God's will is known by dreams, visions, and 'words of knowledge'.

By contrast with these sadly unbiblical ideas, this book presents the time-honoured, scriptural view that Christians must seek God's will in all the major decisions of life, such as career, marriage, location, and church. Six essential steps are traced from the Bible, and principles are given on additional practical issues such as possessions and leisure activities; ambition and wealth; joining or leaving a church.

Here is a strong challenge to authentic Christian commitment, with an abundance of pastoral advice.

Church Membership in the Bible
61 pages, paperback, ISBN 978 1 870855 64 8

Christ has designed a 'home' or family for his people, described in these pages as an accomplishment of divine genius. This is a magnificent subject, vital to spiritual growth and blessing and also to our service for the Saviour.

This book answers many questions about churches and church membership in New Testament times. Next to having a real walk with Christ and knowing the doctrines of the faith, membership of a good church has a powerful formative influence on the believer's life.

The Faith
Great Christian Truths
119 pages, paperback, ISBN 978 1 870855 54 9

There is nothing like this popular, non-technical sweep through key themes of the Christian faith, highlighting very many inspiring and enlivening points. It often takes an unusual approach to a topic in order to bring out the full wonder and significance. It is designed to be enjoyed by seasoned Christians, and also by all who want to explore the great features of the faith, and discover the life of the soul.

CONTENTS:

The Mysterious Nature of a Soul	The New Birth
What God is Actually Like	Why the Resurrection?
The Fall of Man	Prophecies of Resurrection
The Three Dark Hours of Calvary	The Holy Trinity

Not Like Any Other Book
Interpreting the Bible
161 pages, paperback, ISBN 978 1 870855 43 3

Faulty Bible interpretation lies at the root of every major mistake and 'ism' assailing churches today, and countless Christians are asking for the old, traditional and proven way of handling the Bible to be spelled out plainly.

A new approach to interpretation has also gripped many evangelical seminaries and Bible colleges, an approach based on the ideas of unbelieving critics, stripping the Bible of God's message, and leaving pastors impoverished in their preaching.

This book reveals what is happening, providing many brief examples of right and wrong interpretation. The author shows that the Bible includes its own rules of interpretation, and every believer should know what these are.

Do We Have a Policy?
Paul's Ten Point Policy for Church Health & Growth
93 pages, paperback, ISBN 978 1 870855 30 3

What are our aims for the shaping of our church fellowship, and for its growth? Do we have an agenda or framework of desired objectives? The apostle Paul had a very definite policy, and called it his 'purpose', using a Greek word which means – a plan or strategy displayed for all to see.

This book sets out ten policy ideals, gleaned from Paul's teaching, all of which are essential for the health and growth of a congregation today.

Worship in the Melting Pot
148 pages, paperback, ISBN 978 1 870855 33 4

'Worship is truly in the melting pot,' says the author. 'A new style of praise has swept into evangelical life shaking to the foundations traditional concepts and attitudes.' How should we react? Is it all just a matter of taste and age? Will churches be helped, or changed beyond recognition?

This book presents four essential principles which Jesus Christ laid down for worship, and by which every new idea must be judged.

Here also is a fascinating view of how they worshipped in Bible times, including their rules for the use of instruments, and the question is answered – What does the Bible teach about the content and order of a service of worship today?

Physicians of Souls
The Gospel Ministry
285 pages, paperback, ISBN 978 1 870855 34 1

'Compelling, convicting, persuasive preaching, revealing God's mercy and redemption to dying souls, is seldom heard today. The noblest art ever granted to our fallen human race has almost disappeared.'

Even where the free offer of the Gospel is treasured in principle, regular evangelistic preaching has become a rarity, contends the author. These pages tackle the inhibitions, theological and practical, and provide powerful encouragement for physicians of souls to preach the Gospel. A vital anatomy or order of conversion is supplied with advice for counselling seekers.

The author shows how passages for evangelistic persuasion may be selected and prepared. He also challenges modern church growth techniques, showing the superiority of direct proclamation. These and other key topics make up a complete guide to soulwinning.

The Baptist Confession of Faith 1689
Edited by Peter Masters
53 pages, paperback, ISBN 978 1 870855 24 2

C. H. Spurgeon said of this great Confession – 'Here the youngest members of our church will have a body of Truth in small compass, and by means of the scriptural proofs, will be able to give a reason of the hope that is in them.' This brilliant summary of doctrine (in the same family as the Westminster Confession), with its invaluable proof texts, is here gently modernised in punctuation, with archaic words replaced. Explanations of difficult phrases have been added in italic brackets. A brief history of the Confession, with an index, is included.

The Charismatic Illusion
Co-author: John C. Whitcomb
100 pages, paperback, ISBN 978 1 908919 70 0

Now with more answers to questions asked by people investigating the arguments, this veteran book contends for the biblical position on the gifts that prevailed for nearly 2,000 years before the charismatic movement came along.

Here is the dynamic teaching of the Spirit that sustained true churches and believers through dark and bright years of history, through the Reformation, through the Puritan era, through the time of great Confessions of Faith, through repeated awakenings and revivals, and through the worldwide growth of the modern missionary movement.

Here is the case for authentic biblical spiritual life.

The Healing Epidemic
143 pages, paperback, ISBN 978 1 908919 24 3

Dr Masters here answers the arguments used by healers in support of their methods. He explains Bible teaching on what demons can and cannot do, and how *James 5* should be implemented in churches today. He also proves that the conscious mind should always be switched on for spiritual activities. Included is a brilliant assessment of miraculous healing by a leading British medical professor.

'This volume is a masterful analysis and criticism of the most recent manifestations of charismatic phenomena . . . The exposition of *James 5.13-14* is excellent, and his analysis of the place of the mind in the Christian's experience is remarkable.' – *Bibliotheca Sacra*

Only One Baptism of the Holy Spirit
109 pages, paperback, ISBN 978 1 870855 17 4

Young Christians these days are confronted by much confusion on the teaching of the Holy Spirit and how he baptises, fills and anoints God's people. Contradictory statements and clashing ideas flow from a new generation of anecdotal-style books.

When is the believer baptised with the Spirit, and what does it amount to? Is there a second baptism? How exactly does the Spirit witness with our spirit? How does assurance come? Is the believer to struggle against sin, or does the Lord fight the battle for him? What is the filling of the Spirit? Clear answers are given to all such questions, with 'proof texts'. Ideal for all, especially young believers and study groups.

Joshua's Conquest
Was it Moral? What Does It Say to Us Today?
119 pages, paperback, ISBN 978 1 870855 46 4

This is a book for reading, rather than a commentary. Its aim is to bring out the spiritual message of the *Book of Joshua* for today, and also to explain some of the 'problem' portions and passages which evoke questions on, for example, the morality of so much killing, and whether God was responsible for hardening the hearts of the Canaanites.

The Mutual Love of Christ & His People
An explanation of the *Song of Solomon* for personal devotions and Bible study groups
115 pages, paperback, ISBN 978 1 870855 40 2

The courtship of the *Song of Solomon* provides fascinating scenes and events designed to show the love of Christ for his redeemed people, and theirs for him. Prophecies of Christ abound. Here, also, are lessons for Christians when they become cold or backslidden, showing the way to recover Christ's presence in their lives.

Heritage of Evidence
127 pages, 135 colour illustrations, paperback, ISBN 978 1 908919 71 7

The British Museum holds a huge number of major discoveries that provide direct corroboration and background confirmation for an immense sweep of Bible history. This illustrated survey of Bible-authenticating exhibits has been designed as a guide for visitors, and also to give pleasure and interest to readers unable to tour the galleries.

Hallmarks of Christian Character
135 pages, paperback, ISBN 978 1 908919 80 9

Here are great themes for the Christian life, combining devotional, encouraging and practical views of the distinctive characteristics, aims and way of thinking of sincere believers.

Beginning with the foundation of humility, these pages show the strong sense of pilgrimage shared by true Christians, their outgoing helpfulness, their sense of closeness to God, their attitude to serving the Lord, their happiness and their access to the power of the Spirit.

The Dark Side of Christian Counselling
E. S. Williams
155 pages, paperback, ISBN 978 1 870855 65 5

It is amazing how rapidly the Christian counselling movement has spread through churches in the UK, teaching that hurts and depressions once considered part of normal life are illnesses to be treated. It implies that for 1900 years the Bible has been insufficient for the woes of God's people, or for their sanctification, but that now we have the 'insights' of anti-Christian psychologists to make good the deficit.

In this book medical doctor Ted Williams challenges these claims, giving a clear-cut and interesting overview of the counselling movement.

His survey of the careers and teaching of the giants of secular psychology, the pillars of its 'faith', is unique. Nowhere else are these great names so clearly critiqued from a Christian point of view, and their militant atheism laid bare. Yet these are the heroes of the new Christian counselling.

Christ or Therapy?
E. S. Williams
157 pages, paperback, ISBN 978 1 870855 71 6

It is not widely realised that there is an irreconcilable difference between the remedies for sadness and grief set out in the Bible, and those put forward by the world of psychotherapy. A gulf also exists between the biblical policy for marriage, and that proposed by secular marriage guidance psychologists. Many well-known evangelical authors and churches, however, have turned entirely to the secular remedies and policies in these matters. This book shows what the differences are, including a remarkable review of depression in the Bible, and its relief.

This is the sequel to *The Dark Side of Christian Counselling.*

For a full listing of Wakeman titles please see www.wakemantrust.org